Understanding the Incarnation
A Candle of Understanding

UNDERSTANDING
the
INCARNATION

A Candle of Understanding

James Atkinson

James Atkinson

deo
PUBLISHING

BLANDFORD FORUM

Theological Seminar series, 4

Published by Deo Publishing
PO Box 6284, Blandford Forum, DT11 1AQ, UK

Copyright © 2008 Deo Publishing

Cover illustration by Bernard Madden

British Library Cataloguing-in-Publication data
A catalogue record for this book is available from the British Library

Printed by Cromwell Press, Trowbridge, Wiltshire

ISSN 1566-2098
ISBN 978-1-905679-08-9

Contents

Acknowledgements

I acknowledge with great gratitude the help Susan Smith has given in the preparation of this book. She has prepared the entire MS and procured for me books and information.

Further, my thanks go to the publisher, Dr. David E. Orton, who in sensitive and scholarly fashion has steered the work through the processes of publication.

My thanks also go to my daughter, Mary, for proofreading the text.

All faults and errors are my own.

James Atkinson

Introduction

A few introductory remarks are in order as the reader opens this book.

a. *From Jesus to Christ*

To move from an apprehension of Jesus to a comprehension of him as the Christ, the Christ sent by God "for us and for our salvation," is to make the supreme and ultimate intellectual and spiritual journey of life. Such a pilgrimage creates a new life in the process, a new life with a new mind and spirit, a new way of thinking, a new understanding.

How the disciples grew in this conviction from Jesus to Christ, how the Early Church grew in this conviction, how the three theologians of the New Testament (John, Paul, and the author of Hebrews) explained Christ for all time, constitutes the groundwork of the present study. In short, it is a paradigm for understanding the Incarnation.

On this basis, we are bold enough to suggest what such a christocentric incarnational understanding might mean for the life and witness of the world Church today, indeed for the world religions, not least, for our common everyday life.

b. *The Candle of Understanding*

There is a striking story in the Apocrypha[1] (2 Esdras/*4 Ezra* 14) of a man called Ezra. This Ezra, probably a contemporary of St. Paul,[2] is deeply concerned about the state of the world, how it will all end, and what he should say to his contemporaries about the situation. He is

---

[1] The Apocrypha ('hidden works') is a collection of stories, legends, visions *et al.*, which were excluded from the Jewish canonical scriptures at the Synod of Jamnia (AD 90) but included in the canonical scriptures by Rome at the Council of Trent (1545-47). Protestantism excludes them from the canon, permitting their use for private edification, but granting them no authority in matters of doctrine.

[2] *4 Ezra* (=2 Esdras) is commonly dated to the first century AD, and there are parallels between its language and Paul's on the subject of divine revelation.

troubled, meditating on these matters, sitting under an oak tree, with his eyes fixed on a particular bush. In his meditation, or dream or vision, God addresses him out of this bush. God says to him, that it was out of a bush that he spoke to Moses (Exod 3.2-8) and revealed himself; now, in like manner, out of a bush, he is addressing Ezra. (This at once sets Ezra's experience and message on the highest possible level as divine revelation and not the mere reflections of a holy man meditating under an oak tree.)

In his message God first reminds Ezra of how he had led Israel out of their bondage in Egypt to the Promised Land; how he had given Moses the Law, and had revealed to him secrets of the times, some of which he was to declare, some of which were to remain secret. And he had a similar message for Ezra.

Ezra is to lay up in his heart the signs God has already given in history, as well as his present visions and dreams, with God's interpretation of them. He is to live in a company of like-minded believers who understand these things. The world is divided, its future uncertain, and threatening. He was to set his house in order, remove corruption, strengthen the faithful, and support the weak. He is to dismiss all worldly thought and turn exclusively to spiritual matters. God warns him that greater and worse evils are to descend on the earth. And he adds: "Truth had fled from the earth."

Ezra promises complete obedience. He says that the Law has been burnt, and nobody knows or understands these things any more; the world knows nothing of these things. He begs God to give him his Holy Spirit so that he can understand these matters and write down these things that God is telling him, including the Law, so that these people may live and not die in ignorance.

In reply, God advises him to collect together some chosen scribes, together with the necessary writing material, and in total isolation write down all that God has said.

And now comes the point of this story for the present book. God takes Ezra aside and in a kind of warm confidentiality says to him:

> "I shall light in your heart a candle of understanding,
> which shall not be put out, until the things are finished."

This book seeks a profounder understanding of Christ; of truths we seem somehow to have half-forgotten; of what God has to say about Jesus, his Christ; and of God's own 'candle of understanding in the heart'. This candle, in the form of this book, is now offered to my readers.

So let us proceed in our quest to understand Christ more deeply, more truly, more divinely - as God intended him to be understood.

It needs a Milton to express this thought. In the last book of *Paradise Lost*, after Adam and Eve (our first parents) had lost the Paradise which God had intended for humankind, for in their disobedience they had estranged themselves from God, Milton refers to our "lingering parents" looking back to Paradise, now lost, "so late their happy seat":

> Some natural tears they dropped, but wiped them soon:
> The world was all before them, where to choose
> Their place of rest, and Providence their guide;
> They hand in hand with wandring steps and slow,
> Through Eden took their solitary way.   (XII 645ff.)

But, a little earlier, Adam had received the angelic promise of the Redeemer's presence and the Holy Spirit which he would 'send along', and though leaving Paradise

> … thou … shalt possess
> A paradise within thee, happier far. (XII 586ff.)

In and through all the sorrows and tragedies of his life, even the loss of his sight, a tragedy indeed to a writer, a thinker and reader and man of letters, Milton cherished the light that burned within his mind and heart, the light of "Paradise within thee," the angelic promise of Christ within him, the light which I have just said will never be put out, "a candle of understanding in the heart."

c. *Explaining the Inexplicable*
(i) *The inadequacy of normal, reasonable everyday language*

We face superhuman difficulties in seeking to understand the Incarnation. Seeking to understand creation, the Big Bang, why there is life at all, what it means, what is the purpose, are but child's play in comparison with trying to understand the Incarnation. The reason is that it involves a totally different category of thought, a dimension of thought which does not come naturally to humankind, but has to be given (revealed) as an aid, like a lamp or torch given to us to help us see our way during a blackout.

Reflect on this fact: it took Jesus twenty years to understand his own nature and the divine role God intended for him. We see this from the age of thirteen, when he deserted the village crowds and was eventually found sitting in the Temple with the learned priests and scholars, listening to them and asking them questions: from that day, perhaps even earlier, till his final visit to Jerusalem twenty years later, when he wept at the Holy City's refusal to accept him, and where he was finally crucified. Also during those twenty years, right through the long Temptation in the wilderness and under continual temptations, in permanent prayer, day and night, he begged God his Father to make clear his nature and destiny, and what God required of him to fulfil his nature and destiny.

Simply ask yourself, if it took Jesus himself twenty years to understand who he was and what was the purpose God intended for him, are you likely to understand the Incarnation in its depth and reality by the mere reading of this all too shallow book, or even by your own study and reflection?

Consider further, how the genius St. Paul, in the intensity of his determination to destroy any ideas of Christ's divine nature, actually broke down - to find the Truth in Christ whom he was cruelly persecuting, and in that breakdown, to find his divine role and destiny. Note carefully the opposition he experienced at the hands even of the Apostles. But not only that: in all his missionary work, one of his greatest obstacles was the way in which his hearers resisted the Incarnation, and were determined to accommodate Paul's exclusive christocentric thinking ("other foundation can no man lay") to their way of thinking. Here we refer to the Judaizers, the Ebionites, the mystics, the Gnostics and all those who would limit the theology of the Incarnation to their own human preconceptions (these views are discussed in their place in the text of the present book).

(ii) *The necessity of biblical and creedal language*
All such loose, free thinking (I would simply call it non-biblical), described by church historians as heretical, went on till the time of young Athanasius, the brilliant young scholar whom the bishop of Alexandria took along to the Council of Nicea, in 325, as his secretary and advisor.

It was at Nicea that the Church Fathers, after much controversy and debate, invented the word *homo-ousios*, "of the same substance," to clinch the debate on Christ's nature, that he was of the same essence or being as God. The word aroused and still arouses debate and controversy, but orthodoxy has stuck with it, and the word abides in our creeds. But in fact we have no words to define or even express God and his activity. Our words are but pointers, guides, true indications from the Holy Spirit, given to guide the Church, to keep us from drowning in the swamps of our own human finitude.

Athanasius (c. 297-373) is of decisive importance in seeing how Christianity formulated its understanding of Christ, his nature, being and God-given mission to the world. True, the Nicene Creed of 325 was imposed on a number of "neutrals" and malcontents, who were to give Athanasius and the orthodox much trouble later. It was only when the three great Cappodocian Fathers[3] later weighed into the disputes, that Athanasius's theology was vindicated.

He was four times exiled by the emperors, deposed by his bishop, but single-mindedly and single-handedly, in office or in exile, pursued his mission. He had been much loved as a young rector of a parish in Alexandria, and was as highly educated in secular learning as in theological learning. So deep was the love of the people, that they actually publicly lynched his successor, the imposed bishop of Alexandria, to let the authorities know what they thought of their beloved Athanasius. In exile he would be found among his desert monks sitting simply, like them, on a rush mat with a bundle of papyrus leaves beside him, writing Festal Letters to his people, and profound theological works for the world to explain Christ. He never faltered or failed, and Christianity can be thankful that he was given, in his closing years, grace and peace as the devoted "pastoral bishop" to fulfil his abiding mission.

He wrote chiefly for a true *biblical* understanding of the Incarnation and against all Judaizers, Arians of all shades of opinion (unitarians and half-believers), pagans and all who would set up Christ among the semi-gods. This majestic figure, this "invisible patriarch," flourished in all circumstances, almost like St. Paul. In the deep stillness of the desert, in its intense light, he wrote letters, and books of abiding significance, but we must confine ourselves for this enquiry to the light he shows in his costly defence of the true meaning of the Incarnation.

With unflagging energy he devoted his life to the truth of the *homo-ousion* formula. He argued that the formula expressed this truth:

> If Christ is God, then he must be God in the same sense as God the Father is God. Divinity is one substance.

To believe in the divinity of the Son in any other way is to introduce paganism "with its ranks of divinities, semi-divinities, demi-semi-divinities," as Bettenson expressed it.[4] How then can we maintain that the Father is one God, the Son is God, and the Holy Spirit is God, and

[3] The three brilliant leaders of philosophical Christian orthodoxy in the late fourth century, namely Gregory of Nazianzus, Basil of Caesarea, and his brother Gregory, bishop of Nyssa.

[4] See below.

at the same time safeguard Christian monotheism? There is only one essential "stuff" of Godhead. True, we experience, and Scripture teaches three "persons," three hypostases, three objective realities which – or rather who – have relations with each other and with man, though not independently of each other. All other ways of thinking (which means all the heresies) would have the effect of paganizing Christianity, and offering paganistic intellectualism. He never yielded in this vision. By pen and word, through all difficulties and dangers, he taught and preached One God One Saviour. In this insight and by his sheer invincible spirit, he safeguarded Christianity from disintegration, perhaps dissolution, and preserved the unity and integrity of the Christian faith.

It was a percipient insight when Adolf Harnack (1856-1930), the mighty German historian, described Luther as joining hands with Athanasius over the centuries. As Athanasius safeguarded the Incarnation in his day, so Luther restored the centrality of Christ, both to the understanding of the Bible as well as a true christology which set the Reformation on fire. As a student, I recall my old professor, Oliver Quick, maintaining that all modern christologies find their origin in Luther, in his evangelical theology. It was a profound insight, and has remained with me these last seventy-odd years.[5]

Allow me to offer a short extract on the subject of God and Man, from his classic work *On the Incarnation*:

I. GOD AND MAN

(*a*) *Creation and the Fall: Man Mortal by Nature, Immortal by Grace*
[*Three erroneous views of creation are rejected: (i) the Stoic 'spontaneous generation'; (ii) the Platonic notion of pre-existent matter; (iii) the Gnostic idea of the 'Demiurge', the agent of creation, other than the Father. In contrast to these is the Christian doctrine:*] The godly teaching and the faith according to Christ ... knows that God made the whole order of things and brought it into being out of nothing ... [Gen. i. 1; Heb. xi. 3 *and* 'the most useful book of the Shepherd', i.e. *Hermas* (Mandate I)]. For God is good, or rather he is in himself the source of goodness. Being good, he could not grudge anyone anything; therefore he did not grudge existence to any; and so he made all things out of nothing through his own Word, our Lord Jesus Christ. And among created things he felt special concern for the race of men, and since he observed that according to the condition of their birth men were incapable of permanence, he bestowed on them a further gift. He did not merely create man in the same way as he created all the irrational creatures on earth; he made men 'after his own image', giving them a share in the power of his own Word,[1] so that they might have as it were shadows of the

Word, and thus becoming 'rational', might be able to continue in blessedness and live the true life, which is the life of the saints in paradise. In short, Athanasius is saying that the divine, historical revelation in Jesus of Nazareth gives to humankind a complete and total rationality of human nature, in contrast to the limited, merely human speculation of the philosophers.

But God also knew that man's will could incline either way, and therefore in his providence he safeguarded the grace given to man by imposing a condition and putting him in a certain place. For he brought them to his own paradise, and laid down this condition; that if they preserved the grace and remained good, they should have a life in a paradise free from trouble, pain, and care, besides having the promise of immortal life in heaven: but if they transgressed and turned away and became evil, they should know that they would suffer that corruption in death which was natural to them, and then they would no longer live in paradise, but outside it; therefore they would remain in death and corruption when they died.

For 'to die in death'[2] surely means just this, not merely to die but to remain in the corruption of death.

De Incarnatione, 3

---

[1] Cf. *Contra Arianos*, iii. 10 (*ad fin.*) ... We are called 'the image and glory of God' not on our own account; it is on account of the image and true glory of God that dwells in us, namely his Word who later became flesh for us, that we have the grace of this designation.

[2] Gen. ii. 16. Edition: Migne, *Patrologia Graeca*, xxv-xxviii (reprinting Benedictine text of 1698). Henry Bettenson, *The Early Christian Fathers*, 1956, pp. 377f.

(iii) *Knowing the truth and doing the truth*

Following these rather minatory thoughts, there is one final warning which I address both to myself and to the reader. The apologist is always in the great danger of thinking that when he has explained a theological issue, the matter is settled. But it is not. The final issue in all explanations, is not simply to explain it in words, but that both the writer and reader have each translated the words, true and accurate though they be, into a deep appropriation and experience of their meaning in the very depths of their soul and mind. And still more important, and in itself, heartening, this meaning and this depth do not *require* or *demand* a theological explanation before they can be experienced. All that is required is a humble heart. The peasant may know what the philosopher could never understand, just as the common people heard Jesus gladly, though the scholars and priests were bewildered. But when Christianity is challenged, the reader may have firm grounds for his or her belief, as well as answers to his or her own questions. And that is why I have written this book. If you know these things, happy are you if you do them. It is less a question of knowing the truth; more a question of doing the truth. "Those that do what is true come to the light" (see Jn 3.32; 13.17).

After these introductory reflections, let us begin our study of the meaning of the Incarnation for us today, and in that fresh understanding, know what Christ meant when he said to the bewildered, incredulous Pilate questioning him on his identity:

> For this I was born,
> and for this I came into the world,
> to testify to the truth.
> Everyone who belongs to the truth listens to my voice. (Jn 18.37)
>
> Heaven itself echoes:
> "Listen to him!"

An example of distinguishing between the knowing of a truth expressed abstractly in terms of concepts on the one hand and knowing the living dynamic of simply living the truth, in life (simply expressed by Christ as "Follow me"), will be found in Chapter 8. Here I have expressed what is normally called Christian vocation as discipleship. I have deliberately spoken in terms of practical discipleship, following Jesus, and avoided the abstract word vocation. Similarly, earlier in the book (Chapter 3) I refer to Christ's use of the word "faith" not as abstract belief, as a noun, but always as a verb, an activity, something one does, not something one knows.

All abstract nouns, though necessary and useful for argument and discussion, when used to describe God's dynamic activity in the world, stultify our minds because they compel the mind to think in static terms and concepts. Even the word Incarnation expresses a static thought. Our great forefathers in framing our creeds never used abstract terms. Not "I believe in the Incarnation ...," a phrase which not only opens itself to all kinds of interpretation, but opens the way for all kinds of modernizers, half-believers and diluters of the faith, to interpret the creeds in their own way. No! Not "I believe in the Incarnation," but decisively, "He came down from heaven. And was made man." These phrases leave no room for doubt. We do not read, "I believe in the Resurrection." We read, "The third day he rose again." No degree of intellectual subtlety, no manipulation of abstract terms can affect the plain, direct statements: "He was made man." "The third day he rose again."

Think in terms of verbs rather than nouns - as the Bible does, and as the great Church Fathers did.

(iv) *Christ's claim to forgive sins is to state his divine manhood*

A highly significant fact emerges early in the ministry of Jesus, and that is his claim to forgive sin. In Mark 2 we read that after his first mission of preaching in the synagogues around Nazareth, and healing all manner of sicknesses and diseases, he returns home to Capernaum. We find him sitting at home "preaching the word" to a packed house of villagers among whom are some scribes, doubtless sent to investigate and report on this new movement. Crowds press at the door striving to get in and hear those precious words. Four men come along bearing a paralytic on his pallet. Unable to get near, they ingeniously and determinedly climb up on to the roof by means of the outside staircase, lift off the roof of the house (made of brushwood), and gently lay their crippled friend, almost certainly known to Jesus, right at Jesus' feet as he is preaching. Marvelling at their faith (and ingenuity), Jesus addresses the paralytic in friendly, even affectionate terms, saying, "My son, your sins are forgiven you." These words greatly offend the scribes "sitting there," for according to Jewish teaching, only God, and God alone, has the prerogative to forgive sin. But Jesus makes his point clearly and decisively "… that you may know that the Son of man has authority on earth to forgive sins." Jesus quite clearly identifies his nature and mission with divine authority. We shall develop this in Chapters 1 and 2, for it is highly significant for our understanding of the Incarnation.

This very claim to forgive sin in itself sets Jesus above prophet and priest, above the Mosaic Law, above all Jewish ideas and traditions of messiahship. As the mediator of a far more profound and universal kind of forgiveness, a message and authority from God, Jesus showed himself as the possessor of a strictly divine authority. It is as forgiver of sin, and saviour from the wrath which is the consequence of sin, that Jesus first stands forth in Jewish eyes as a divine person. This means that it was through a doctrine of atonement that Christian Jews felt their way to a fuller understanding of the Incarnation.

Further compelling evidence of the universal validity of this gospel of redemptive forgiveness is given in the first sermon Peter preached at the Feast of Pentecost, immediately after the Resurrection. In Acts 2, we find him addressing the crowds, upbraiding them for their unbelief and for their assenting to the cruel death by crucifixion of God's own messiah, yet in the same breath, offering them the gospel of free forgiveness, and the re-creation of a new life in the loving Christ. It is a staggering witness to the power and meaning of the forgiveness of sin.

This moves us from our study of the Gospel narratives to the life of the Early Church, so dramatically displayed by the converted St. Paul. It was this recognition of the Godhead of the Messiah Jesus which lies at the foundation of Paul's theology. St Paul's message rests upon the fundamental conviction that in the earthly life, death and resurrection of Jesus Christ, God had accomplished a supreme and single act of grace for the deliverance of humankind from the otherwise inevitable consequences of his law. Grace, to St. Paul, meant the free and loving action of God to save and redeem his lost humankind, and for all practical purposes, that meant Christ, his personification, if the reader can accept such strong anthropomorphic language. We should avoid any sense of thinking of Jesus as a holy man, or saint, indeed any sense of seeing Christ as some cult figure. No! Paul presents the life of Christ as the act of the living God as working in love for the delivery of creation from the bondage and corruption of humankind. "God was in Christ reconciling the world to himself" (2 Cor 5.19). God does this entirely out of love for his lost people. "God proves his love for us in that while we still were sinners Christ died for us" (Rom 5.8). In a few words this is the meaning of the Incarnation (see Chapter 4). This is our gospel. Here everything beings to cohere, to make sense. Here we begin, albeit with a human reluctance, to understand the Incarnation, God at work in Jesus of Nazareth, at work for us and our salvation. He never rests. "He neither slumbers nor sleeps."

d. *On Reading this Book: A Word to the Reader*
First, you hold in your hand a book of some 180 pages, some 75,000 words. But these 75,000 words carry a further hundred thousand "hidden" words. They are the references to the Bible. These "hidden" words are infinitely more valuable than anything this author says, and he would like you to consider them as part of his book. They convey the ultimate authority of his study. I suggest that you read them as you read the book. Such reading will keep you in constant touch with the Word of God. As you read the book, God will be reading alongside, even speaking to you.

Second, I argue in the book that in seeking to understand the Incarnation, God active in Christ, we do not have the language to express its meaning, nor the mind to apprehend or comprehend its meaning. I argue that reason cannot lead us to God, even to convince reason, by means of reason, that reason is inadequate for this task. There is a kind of logical blockage. We are dealing with two different categories of thought. Even the disciples found the Incarnation hard to believe, and they had three years of personal tuition. Even at the Ascension, the final occasion they were with Christ, he "upbraided them for their unbelief"

(Mk 16.14). Jewish minds rejected it: Greek minds dismissed it. Modern minds, educated in the liberal tradition of the West, though often sympathetic to the values of Christianity, withdraw at this point. When I argue that reason cannot guide us, I am simply saying what the brilliant French mathematician, Blaise Pascal (1629-1662), meant when he said:

> The heart has its reasons,
> That reason does not know. (*Pensées* 16)

The paradox is that only reason can persuade reason of its own inadequacy. My argument is that the Incarnation is God's way of bridging the gap that lies between man and God. As Pachomius, the first monk (259-346) expressed it:

> When the Lord ceases to reveal himself,
> we are but men, like any other men.

In simple terms: to understand God and his Incarnation, reason needs revelation.

The great Elizabethan reformer and theologian, Henry Bullinger, in his *Decades*, says to his readers:

> Pray earnestly to our bountiful God
> That he will grant to you
> the opening of your ears and mind
> So that in all that I shall say (write).
> The Lord's name be praised
> And your souls profited abundantly.

In such a frame of mind, read this book. If it deepens the understanding of just one reader, the author is rewarded.

Part I
The Incarnation Revealed

1
God, Man, Jesus

a. *Christ's Question to Us: "Who do you say that I am?"*
At the height of his ministry Jesus questioned his disciples, saying, "Who do men say that I am?" After hearing the several views, he then pressed home the decisive, determinative questions, "But, what about you yourselves? Who do you say that I am?" (Mk 8.27-29).

To find the right answer to that question (by "right" I mean the biblical answer), is to attain the ultimate, final truth, which begins to yield a total and entire understanding of Jesus, and derivatively, of God and Man. In turn, this understanding begins to yield rational, working answers to all the questions which confront us in life: sin, evil, death, our ultimate destiny.

Such is the theme of this study: understanding the Incarnation. To effect this, we will argue that after a period of teaching lasting three years, Jesus delivered his disciples from the generally accepted religio-political view of the Messiah (the Christ) as the deliverer of the nation, to the divine view of Christ as the deliverer of humankind from the spiritual bondage of sin into the liberty of freedom in truth. We will seek to consolidate this understanding by turning to the three great theologians of the New Testament, the author of St. John's Gospel, St. Paul and the author of the Epistle to the Hebrews, so that "the eyes of our hearts may be enlightened" (Eph 1.18) and that we may be "strengthened in our inner being" (Eph 1.16). Finally, we are emboldened to indicate how such an understanding of the Incarnation throws fresh light on our present-day situation.

The strength of Christ's historical mission and message, the power in its truth, lies not only in seeing this, but in understanding this and appropriating it to oneself. It is not that you believe it to be true, but that you *know* it is. It is to move into a higher awareness, which I can but describe as certainty. You know that God first revealed to literate humanity (i.e. the Jews) his ways and purpose and the promise of Christ, in and by means of Adam, Abraham, Moses, the prophets, and finally, "when the days were fulfilled," in Jesus of Nazareth.

The story is familiar and hardly needs retelling, but it is important to sketch the history here to understand Christ in his historical setting.

b. *Christ in His Historical Setting*

Adam and Eve (i.e. mankind) were set in a perfect existence with only one single warning: knowledge may bring disaster. The Tempter enters, presumably by divine permission, to persuade Adam that knowledge would bring equality with God. In this delusion Adam disobeys, and consequently, alienated from God, brings disaster upon all posterity. So the Bible explains man's fundamental illusion that his life is his own, and that the world is at his disposal. How else could such a profound, divine truth be stated?

Adam is our father in the human sense, but Abraham is our father in that we are spiritual descendants of him. Abraham was saved by his faith (Gen 16.6), as we are, a promise given to all his descendants, and we are his spiritual descendants. Moses delivered these people from bondage in Egypt to fulfil their religious role, and God promised Moses that he would raise up a prophet like him from among the Jews: "And I will put my words into his mouth, and he shall speak to them all that I command him" (Deut 18.18). To his words all the people were to heed (words echoed in the Baptism of Jesus and in his Transfiguration,[1] as well as in the later prophets).

In the words just quoted, God promised Moses (Deut 18.18) that he would raise up for them a prophet like him from among the Jews, "… and I will put my words in his mouth, and he shall speak to them all that I command him, and him shall you heed." But when he came, tragically for mankind, they did not heed Christ's words, nor the clear witness of John the Baptist, who clearly taught that the Messiah had at last appeared in the form of Jesus of Nazareth. "Listen to him." John the Baptist received the treatment meted out to all prophets. His head was served up at Herod's dining table at the whim of Herod's queen, and by a dancing girl. This is how the world treats God's messengers and prophets.

c. *Christ Always Points to God*

The prophet promised was Jesus of Nazareth. But it is important at this point to make clear that Christianity is not a Jesus cult. Christianity restores and completes an abiding true faith in God that withstands all the

[1] See Chapter 2 (p. 000).

evil, all the problems, all the negative hostilities that hurl themselves (by God's permission) against us frail mortals. But still more, in understanding this Jesus, we are further given a foretaste of eternal life in the here and now, as "a first instalment" (2 Cor 1.22) and thereby, a sure and certain hope of life with God when we shed this mortal frame. As Jesus said, and note the solemnity and gravity of the opening words, "Very truly [verily, verily] I tell you, whoever believes has eternal life" (Jn 6.47).

Note that Christ always points beyond himself to God, i.e. the God of all creation, the God of all mankind, through our space/time dimension, and indeed through all religion and religions to existential and eternal truth – to God.

Central and determinative as Jesus is to Christianity, faith does not rest in Jesus but in God who sent him and commissioned him. In the Temple itself he "cried out" in an imploring tone, "whoever believes in me believes not in me but in him who sent me" (Jn 12.44). John in his Gospel makes this basic to Christ's mission and purpose. Again, "Very truly, I tell you, whoever receives one whom I send receives me; and whoever receives me receives him who sent me" (Jn 13.20). Matthew says the same, "whoever welcomes you welcomes me, and whoever welcomes me welcomes the one who sent me" (Mt 10.40); Luke, too (Lk 9.48).

In a similar way we tend to misunderstand the parables, and need to note carefully the point that Jesus makes, not what we make of the story. For example, the parable of the Prodigal Son is a total misnomer. The parable is not about a selfish, self-centred young man who wants his share of his inheritance while he can enjoy it. The word "prodigal" does not even appear in the parable. It is about a father who receives back such a son who has wasted his substance and ultimately has only one place to go, his father.

All of us have ultimately one place to go: our Father.

To reject this truth is not to believe that his words are true. Not to walk in his light is to choose to live in ignorance. It is to live in a desert of twilight and to die in shady uncertainty. Christ does not condemn such unbelievers to this shady kingdom. They are self-condemned, a truth they will one day learn, even if only on the Last Day, for his words are not his own, but those of God. He did not come to condemn the world, but to save the world (though it may incur condemnation, before it is saved) (Jn 3.17).

d. *The Holy Spirit*
It is important at this point to recall Jesus' teaching on the Holy Spirit. He clearly taught the disciples at their Last Supper that, though he had

to leave them to fulfil his ministry, it was not as bereft orphans he would leave them, for if they believed his teaching, God and he would come and dwell in their heart and mind, and live in them. Do we realise the meaning of this staggering and stupendous truth? How many of us reflect on and absorb and live by these simple statements, the promise that God and Christ will make their abode and dwell in us, to guide, stimulate, enlarge and reveal, and direct our finite minds and frail hearts into the full truth of life. If you understand my words, go out to the moors and cry out to God "Eureka!" Go out to the seaside and shout to the sea and sky, "I see! Once I was blind, but now I see!" No person, no experience can ever take God from you, nothing can ever separate you from this living and loving God.

To see (understand) Jesus is to see and understand the Father, because he is in the Father and the Father in him. Here is the fundamental truth of Christianity. To see this truth, to understand and appropriate this truth is to say that whoever believes this will not live in darkness, in uncertainty, but will live in the light. As Jesus said (note again the "very truly"): "Very truly, I tell you, whoever believes has eternal life" (Jn 6.47).

What Jesus was saying in words of one, sometimes two, syllables, is that this truth is the basic ground truth of existence for mortal man. "Listen to him," said the divine voice. This was the only way they could convey the authority and gravity of this truth, a voice from heaven itself. This is the truth we must hear and safeguard; in his own words, abide in his Word (i.e. God's Word for us and for our salvation). Jesus was at great pains to declare that his words were not his own, but were the commandments of God his Father, who had sent him for this very purpose and gave him what he should declare. His words are the spirit of God and the life of God. They *are* eternal life. Scholars who explain away all this Johannine teaching as a fabrication of the Early Church, argue thus because it is beyond their all too human thinking. If a Church Father could write this, then Christ was otiose. In other words, Christianity is founded not on human speculation but on the divine revelation in Christ. Not to see this, even to fail and falter, is the final and fatal avoidance of the life God freely and lovingly offers to every individual. It is to deny, even defy God.

This is the message of Christianity. This is the living, loving Gospel. This is the Good News of the Kingdom. This is what is at stake.

e. *Christ, Not Christianity*

The reader will readily see that we are not speaking of Christianity, nor of the Christian Church (they will be discussed later at the proper place; see p. 129), but of Christ and his gospel of grace for all men, women and children all the world over. It is at this level that we seek to write, for it is at this level, and this level alone, that the human mind and the human heart will begin to understand Christ and his work and teaching – his meaning for all humankind. Realities and institutions such as Christianity and the Christian Church, honourable and necessary though they be, are merely derivative of the Christ, *God's Idea* (not ours) and further, and most important, at all times subject to his judgment, which always proves their re-creation and their salvation. When that judgment is condemnatory, even hostile, it is the work of God condemning through our conscience our sin and wrong-headedness. It seems hurtful and hostile, but its true meaning and fulfilment is God in Christ by means of the Holy Spirit dwelling in us and working for and on our behalf, re-creating our true selves.

What I am suggesting is, first, a close attention to what John is saying about God and Creation in relation to Jesus and Man (all humankind). Note in particular, his use of the word "we." John does not speak on his own individual authority as a disciple who had seen, heard and handled Jesus, impressive as this was. All this first hand testimony is collectively supported by an inclusive "we." True, it is John the disciple who is writing and recording, bearing witness to these things, but at the end of the Johannine Gospel all the disciples collectively add their authority, saying, "We know that his testimony is true" (Jn 21.24). This was carefully and deliberately written against all the Ebionites with their poverty-stricken views on the Incarnation and their lack of understanding of these world-shattering events; against all the allegorists, mystics, and individualistic interpretations; and against all the Gnostic and spiritualized interpretations of the Christ event, and there were many such, as Acts and Paul record. Here we have the authoritative, authentic, testified account of the inner group of the disciples who were there and witnessed these things; who heard all that he said; saw all that he had done; and who *understood* these things as Christ had explained to them. It is not their own personal view of Christ: "He expounded everything in private to his disciples" (Mk 4.10, 34). This was the account that would stand to the Last Day, when Christ would come as final proof. All this is given support in the book of Acts, where

Luke, a devoted and educated[2] disciple of both Christ and Paul, after submitting a careful, critical and comprehensive account of Christ's ministry, presents a considered record of those early years of Christianity in Jerusalem and the Empire. Here he carefully tells the story of those halcyon days when the Pharisees, many priests and the common people gave their enthusiastic response; he tells also of the tragic turn of events when they met opposition from the council, and the mob murdered Stephen. He recounts how Saul (Paul) supported the mob which stoned Stephen to death, but later, how God was to put the mantle of Stephen over the shoulders of Paul. Saul was the living and terrifying proof that Jewish officialdom had severed all ties with the Christian Jews. Two thousand years later, as far as the Jews are concerned, the relationship is virtually unchanged, but as far as Paul was concerned, the vision of Christ for all people, without distinction or division, was re-created in him by divine authority, even imposition. Luke recounts all this, and tells the story of Paul's mission to the Empire. Paul himself left a substantial legacy of teaching, and to that we will return (Part II) after we have considered St. John's witness (p. 83). John discloses the mind of Christ.

f. *Objectors to the Incarnation*

So far in this chapter we are arguing that the Incarnation offers a total, coherent, rational understanding of God, Jesus, and Man. Before we develop that argument, we are bound to face three objectors, namely, Judaism, Islam, but more important for this book, the educated, liberal mind of today.

Judaism and Islam have resisted any thought of Incarnation from the beginning, essentially on grounds of their monotheism; the modern mind resists on different grounds because it has grown secularized.

Since the present study is devoted to an understanding of the Incarnation, we are bound to make a deeper study of the Great Refusal of the Jews. To this end, we devote Parts I and II of the present work to see how Jesus himself led his followers, in spite of their continuous unbelief, to understand him as the true fulfilment of their scriptures; and in Part III, the theological arguments follow. This is vital to understand the Incarnation. With regard to Islam, very much on all our minds today, I have offered a brief excursus, directed and largely limited to the current situation. As I see it at present, some statement on Islam, the other great monotheistic Semitic faith, is necessarily demanded.

---

[2] Note his fine literary style in his Gospel of Luke and in his book of Acts.

But, by way of clarification at this early stage, I must protest that Christianity is totally, and without qualification, monotheistic, as will be clarified in the text. Christians believe in the one and only God. God, who so loved the people he had created, as to sustain his selected people the Jews with promises, eventually fulfilled in Jesus, sent his only begotten Son, to restore and redeem his wayward people, as promised and written down by a long line of prophets. But Jesus was not only a prophet, but "more than a prophet." Christ, within the limits of humanity, lived the true, divine human life, said and did only what the Father had given him to say and do, and returned to God. It is totally monotheistic, as all the thinkers of the New Testament explain, and as all the Fathers held and aver and the creeds declare: "We believe in one God...." It is simply an intensified monotheism, a completed and fulfilled monotheism. All these assertions are explained in the text to follow though, in that context, I make the plea that we think not in the outdated terms of Jew and Gentile, the Faithful and the Infidel, as we now do, but start, not from our particular prejudices, but with God, the one and only God, and what he has done, and is doing for us. Here we came naturally to the Incarnation, God's Idea. Still monotheistic.

The entire book is directed to modern thinkers in general, and Part III to selected modern thinkers in particular. We all, Jews, Muslims, Christians, alike, face the criticism of the modern educated mind, and it is to this end that the entire book is directed.

The Great Refusal of the Jews in relation to Christ anticipates the same difficulty which contemporary man finds in Christianity. We should never allow ourselves to judge Jewry harshly, nor ever forget that the authorities of Jesus' day permitted him the freedom to preach in their synagogues, to move from village to village to explain his mission, and even to preach daily in their Holy Temple. They gave him a religious trial at the end, and condemned him after giving him the opportunity to explain himself before a full council. It was a senior member of the Sanhedrin who gave his own tomb for the disciples to bury the body of the crucified Jesus. This says a great deal about Judaism, and explains the new Christian movement (as it was later called) as a revived, even a reformed, fulfilled Judaism.[3] The Jewish mind, with its exalted monotheistic theology, just could not accept the very idea of Incarnation - the one stubborn difficulty contemporary man finds, and Muslims, too. And yet, if understood and believed, this solves all the difficulties (see below, p. 113). Judaism, and Islam too, thought Chris-

---

[3] All the 16th-century Reformers were fine Hebraists. Luther found the gospel in Genesis.

tians were atheists. The Roman Empire called them atheists and persecuted them as atheists. It was a long period of misunderstanding, which
continues today. The only answer is a free and living re-examination of
the evidence and a fresh understanding of our words.

At this point we may be allowed a comment on Islam, the other
great religious criticism of Christianity, a movement which is very
much on the mind of Western man, indeed the world at the present
time, and needs a free and open discussion at the highest spiritual and
academic level, with the fullest coverage of the media. Bombs are an
unworthy answer and leave nothing but disaster, death, misery, hope-
lessness and hatred. Every man, woman, youth and child knows this
deep down. "You will know them by their fruits. Are grapes gathered
from thorns, or figs from thistles?" (Mt 7.16).

Six centuries later, Mohammed inspired a quite different reaction.
Tragically (in my view), for the later history of mankind, he arose at a
time when Arabia was in the grip of paganism, and when Christianity
was at its weakest. Its great intellectual and spiritual Church Fathers
had died, and it was in a mortal struggle against Monothelitism[4] and
Iconoclasm.[5] It was unable to offer the appropriate intellectual, historical and religious reply to this fiery, powerful movement, and Islam
simply offered death or conversion. Naturally, more people accepted
the latter. So Islam prevailed, and Christianity disappeared.

Mohammed rose up against his own people on the grounds of their
idolatry, and after terrible and costly trouble and war, finally prevailed.
Here is not the place to retell this story, but the victory of Islam over
the Holy Roman Empire, Christianity and the Near and Far East, is
the greatest success story in all world history. Islam was repulsed in
France by Charles Martel, the grandfather of Charlemagne, in 732, but
after repeated attempts Islam finally conquered Constantinople, the
bastion of the Empire and of Christianity, in 1453. This spelt the end of
the great Holy Roman Empire. In a remarkable, paradoxical way this
gave an impetus to our own European Reformation, in that the monks
and scholars filed west carrying their manuscripts and books (and their

---

[4] A controversial doctrine at that time in the church of the East that there is only
one "energy" or "will" in Christ, both divine and human.

[5] The Iconoclastic controversies brought great disturbance to both the Eastern and
Western Church in the 8th century. The Church never actually made "images" for
devotion and worship, but did make pictures of the Virgin Mary and the saints as aids
to devotion. All such images and pictures were abhorrent to Jew and Muslim alike,
owing to their strict monotheism. This was later to become an issue between Catho-
lics and Protestants in the Reformation of the 16th century and still is, even today.

ideas!) with them. This wretched rout and retreat bore fruit in the
Renaissance. The Muslims were finally defeated at the gates of Vienna
in 1688 by John III of Poland. It was a thousand-year struggle, and is
still unresolved and unnecessary. Mohammed's Holy War against paganism and superstition, and later against the Empire and Christendom,
was a wholly different reaction from that of Judaism.

An illiterate camel driver, though of noble birth, Mohammed first
attacked the idolatry and superstition of his own countrymen, and then
what he thought to be the paganism, idolatry, superstition and wrong
theology of Christianity at a time (as noted above) when Christianity
was at its weakest. He assaulted the Empire and Christianity, not by
reasonable and civilized argument, but by passionate military might. It
was the sword not the word. First, the Holy War was to be won in the
hearts of believers, the inner war; then the believer was empowered to
fight the outer war, against the infidel.[6]

In saying this, I hasten to say at the outset that I equally deplore all
the crusades and wars against Islam, and all the bulls and encyclicals by
which the Popes incited the Christian nations. My mind is wholly
sympathetic with St. Francis, who went over to preach and talk with
the Muslims, not to fight them. And be it said, the Muslims, though
unconverted and unconvinced, had the grace to give him safe conduct
back home with an armed guard to protect him through hostile territory. This is the level of interchange I seek, and which most people
want. Why have we lost this?[7]

g. *Islam and the Incarnation*

I make this excursus on Islam because I consider Islam today has assumed a challenge to the Christian faith greater than the threats of
secularism and atheism. Several books have been published in recent
years, by scholars and experienced journalists, on the nature of this
challenge, but it is difficult to find a common judgment among them.
The present writer thinks the root of the matter goes back 1300 years
to Mohamet himself, and that fundamentally it is a religious and theo-

---

[6] Jihad - Holy War: the prevalent claim, that the jihadist suicide terrorist of today
earns an immediate access to paradise as martyr on the merit of his bloody, murderous
deeds, is repugnant alike to true religion and to common sense. The true meaning of
the word "martyr" is one who "bears witness": normally for one's faith in times of
persecution, to the point of death. A martyr never takes life, but offers his/her own.

[7] See M.J. Akbar, *The Shade of Swords: Jihad and the Conflict between Islam and Terror-
ism* (Routledge, 2002) for a fine and detailed (though most disturbing) study of the
Muslim mind and its attitude to the Western mind and customs. The work is essentially a detailed history of jihad (Holy War) from Mohammed to the present day.

logical matter. That is why historians, journalists, even politicians eschew or do not understand the real issue, which is theological and religious, and tend to skirt round the problem and handle its symptoms, not its true nature. The author offers this brief excursus on Islam with some hesitation, but feels that in a study of the Incarnation for today, it would be irresponsible not to discuss the Islamic point of view, as well as the Jewish, which gave birth to Christianity. Different historic occasions produce varying expressions of this original intuitive hostility, but I see them as variations on the traditional hostility. Below I refer to a positive way of meeting this problem.

Of the books referred to above, the weighty, authoritative study of the London professor, Efraim Karsh, *Islamic Imperialism*,[8] betrays in its striking title the nature of his argument. He argues that from inception, Islam was imperialist, a creed that made no separation between temporal and religious. It never occurred to Mohammed that he should or could rule in the hearts of men. He set out to conquer the Arab world, and laid down principles for all conquest everywhere.

How unlike Christ: Christ despised Herod and would not deign to speak to him. To Pilate, asking about his kingship, he dismissed the question saying, "My kingdom is not of this world: if it were, my followers would be fighting " (Jn 18.36).

A further contrast is that Jesus' final commission to the apostles was to go out into all the world and preach the gospel to every creature, whereas Mohammed's final address explicitly justified the sword, saying, "Fight all men until they say, 'There is no God but Allah'." (After the attack by air on Washington and New York, Osama bin Laden quoted these words to justify that attack.) Conquest is the heartbeat of Islam.

The Prophet said, "The survival of my community rests on the hooves of its horses and the points of its lances, as long as they keep from tilling the fields. Once they begin to do that, they will become as other men."

Karsh argues that Islam provides Muslim leaders not only with a justification for their violence, but also with a permanent excuse. They can always blame things on the infidel, and at the same time conceal their real aims under the mantle of the Prophet.

The texts quoted in support of his thesis include: "I was ordered to fight all men until they say 'There is no God but Allah'" (Mohammed's final address to his followers, 632). "I shall cross the sea to their islands to pursue them until there remains no one on the face of the earth who

[8] Efraim Karsh, *Islamic Imperialism: A History* (Yale University Press, 2006).

does not acknowledge Allah" (Saladin, 1189). "We will export our revolution throughout the world ... the calls 'There is no God but Allah' and 'Muhammad is the messenger of Allah' are echoed all over the world" (Ayotollah Khomeini, 1979). "I was ordered to fight the people until they say, 'There is no God but Allah'" (Osama bin Laden, 2001).

In the epilogue of his masterly study, Karsh declares that the present hostility to America is only because American world power blocks Arab and Islamic imperialist aspirations, and therein makes itself the natural target for aggression. He writes:

> Osama bin Laden and other Islamists' war ... is the most recent manifestation of the millenarian jihad for a universal Islamic empire (or umma). This is a vision by no means confined to an extremist fringe of Islam, as illustrated by the overwhelming support for the 9/11 attack throughout the Arab and Islamic worlds.
>
> In the historical imagination of many Muslims and Arabs, bin Laden represents nothing short of the new incarnation of Saladin. The House of Islam's war for world mastery is a traditional, indeed venerable, quest that is far from over. Only when the political elites of the Middle East and Muslim world reconcile themselves to the reality of state nationalism, foreswear pan-Arab and pan-Islamic dreams, and make Islam a matter of private faith rather than a tool of political ambition, will the inhabitants of these regions at last be able to look forward to a better future free of would-be Saladins.[9]

Karsh and Akbar (see nn. 8 and 7), in their excellent studies, present an invaluable, historical, factual perspective to our present day situation, but together they provide a grave warning of the dangerous situation the whole world now faces. None of the writers discussed seems to offer a humane, kind, positive way forward. The outlook is bleak. The whole world cries out for some fresh creative thinking, some activation that would forge a new tolerant, humane understanding, a new world brotherhood. Christ offered this. St. Paul travelled the Empire to explain it. The great Church Fathers taught it. Why have we half-forgotten these truths? Why do we lack the will?

One of the many errors and misunderstandings which Islam entertains against what it describes as the degraded and debased "West," is to assume that Western civilisation and culture are expressive of Christianity. They are not. Unlike Islam, Christianity does not believe in any kind of theocentric state. It is a gross perversion to confuse the state with Christianity. The state is a necessary and beneficial order (of di-

---

[9] Efraim Karsh, *Islamic Imperialism*, p. 234.

vine authority in New Testament terms) to maintain justice, law and order, and peace in a fallen, corrupt, sinful world, as St. Paul clearly expressed Christ's mind in Romans 13. But this Divine Order is exercised by sinful men and women. The sharpest and most perceptive critics of Western civilization are Christian men and women. The state and religion are two wholly different categories of thought, which should never be confused. We shall return to this matter in our concluding section where we discuss possible ways of understanding and resolving this matter.

Jason Eliot,[10] a distinguished journalist with an intimate knowledge of the personalities and events of the Middle East (Iran in particular), a linguist and an admirer of the culture of Islam, especially its magnificent architecture, as well as its art and literature, offers a much needed emphasis on the culture of Islam, but seems at a loss to explain how such a culture should yield the Islamic militancy we experience today. He attributes much of this to the alarming growth in population, creating large numbers of rebellious children and young people who feel unwanted and with nowhere to go.

Charles Glass,[11] an American journalist and broadcaster, offers the thesis that Arab countries are simply "tribes with flags," and attributes much of our trouble to the unfair and mistaken creation of nation states in the Middle East by the settlement after the Great War 1914 - 18, in the Balfour Declaration, which led to the creation of all these states, including Israel. He sees everywhere the burden of population growth and weak leadership in all these created states.

This is how most of us think and feel, and even, after all their experience and research and writing, we are left where we were. One reads of a middle-aged financial expert, practising in London, formerly a Christian, now converted to Islam and become a member of a hard-thinking, radical, jihadist group. Here is no radical youth rebelling at our secularized culture. Anecdotal evidence seems to inform us that there are thousands of such converts in Europe and America. It is difficult to understand. Then I recall in my student days in Germany I could never understand why such intelligent people could support the Nazi programme. I asked them, were they just allowing the dictator to tie their hands to stop them trembling? We all know to our bitter sorrow and horrible cost where such thinking landed the whole world.

I read in *Time* magazine of a *private* email which a science professor of Michigan State University sent to the chairman of the Muslim Stu-

---

[10] Jason Eliot, *Mirrors of the Unseen: Journeys in Iran* (Picador, 2006).
[11] Charles Glass, *The Tribes Triumphant* (Harper Collins, 2006).

dents Association who were making a public protest about the Danish cartoons which portrayed the Prophet Mohammed as a "terrorist"; in the course of this email, the professor said to the leader of the protest:

> I am offended not by cartoons, but by more mundane things like behead-
> ing of civilians, cowardly attacks on public buildings, suicide murders,
> murders of Catholic priests (the latest in Turkey), burnings of Christian
> churches, the continued persecution of Coptic Christians in Egypt, the
> imposition of Shariah law on non-Muslims, the rapes of Scandinavian
> girls and women called "whores" in your culture, the murder of film Di-
> rectors in Holland, and the rioting and looting in Paris.

He asked the Muslims to be aware of what he and many of his colleagues thought of their protest.

In Part III of this book I endeavour to make suggestions of a positive nature on how together we may reconsider the matter.

Jason Burke,[12] a journalist of the *Observer*, has a striking experience of first-hand involvement in the struggles of the Middle East. His search is in pursuit of "a general theory of Islamic militancy." He is impressed by the power and effect of Bin Laden's propaganda machine, but concludes that it has not yet set the Islamic world ablaze. He found everywhere the jihadists deploring the moral pollution of the West. He could not find "a general theory of Islamic militancy" – too many countries, too many motivations, too many difficulties.

It so happened that at the time the present writer was noting the point of Burke's thesis, that Islamic militancy was too complex to offer one simple explanation, Pope Benedict XVI was at the University of Regensburg delivering a lecture on Faith, Reason and the University. In that lecture, a very learned, scholarly address, he made the argument that just as Faith and Reason lived harmoniously in the academic milieu of a university, so should this profound sense of coherence prevail in all our everyday activities, not least in religion.

In this context he referred to a book he had recently read, recording a discussion between the highly erudite Byzantine emperor, Manuel II Palacologus, and a very learned Persian Muslim scholar, in the winter barracks near Ankara in 1391. In this conversation the emperor touched on the theme of holy war, and said, "There is no compulsion in religion" (quoting the Qur'an, sura 2.256). The emperor brusquely said to the Persian, "Show me just what Mohammed brought that is new in religion, and there you will find things only evil and inhuman, such as his command to spread by the sword the faith he preached."

---

[12] Jason Burke, *On the Road to Kandahar* (Allen Lane, 2006).

The emperor went on to argue that "spreading the faith by violence was unreasonable ... To convince a reasonable soul, one does not need a strong arm, or weapons of any kind, or any other means of threatening a person with death." The Persian explains that according to Muslim teaching God is absolutely transcendent, his will is not bound up by any of our categories of thought, even that of rationality. The Persian quotes an Islamic scholar who went even further and argued that God is not bound even by his own word.

To the modern reader, this must appear an ancient, abstruse theological argument. However, because it sheds light on the understanding of the Incarnation, I seek here to express it in modern language. The emperor is saying to the Persian scholar that over the centuries Islam has contributed nothing to religious thought other than jihad, Holy War, which means aggression, militancy, fanaticism and wars. In this, the emperor notes, Islam errs. All that reasonable people want is understanding, peace and brotherhood, never war, not even Holy War. The Persian scholar cannot refute this, but pleads that Islamic scholars had already perceived this, and had offered the mitigating argument that God is greater than his word, above whatever man thinks or reasons about his word. The Persian's argument amounts to this: that all such difficulties are resolved by attributing events to Fate; it is the will of Allah. To the Christian emperor, such an argument was untenable, as it is to all Christians, and Jews.

The next day I woke to find that the entire Islamic world was in a state of uproar. The present author knows the Pope, arising from their mutual membership of L'Académie Internationale des Sciences Religieuses, and further, has studied his writings, and in conversation and discussion with him, knows him to be a first-rate, fair-minded informed scholar who would never knowingly hurt anybody of another religion. He is also well read on the subject of the Islamic faith, and has since apologized for causing offence. He cannot of course, withdraw the facts of history.

It is all a very regrettable episode, for the lecture was directed not at Islam but at the West for its all too prevalent attitude that religion is simply a matter of opinion, outside the sphere of rationality. The Pope concluded his lecture with an appeal "to our partners in the dialogue of cultures", a new dialogue between the sciences, religions and cultures, and the chief of all, the Incarnation. The present author makes a similar appeal in Chapter 9, where he deals with the new hopeful atmosphere created by the New Physics.

After this miserable episode, the atmosphere is inauspicious. Does it mean that one can have a conversation with Islam only on Muslim terms? I hope not. Such a conversation would not be a dialogue but a monologue.

h. *Understanding the Incarnation*

What the Incarnation means is that insofar as he is from the Father and of the Father, Christ's own description of himself, we humans find in him as much of the Divine that we as humans could ever understand and experience. In short, we see God. Only Christ can raise our human minds to this divine level of cognition. He is the perfect mediator, our only go-between, our only revelation of God to humans. From heaven, he brings heaven and earth together, in human terms, the only terms we can understand.

Paul was acutely aware of the necessity of holding fast to the belief in the Incarnation. It was towards the end of his life, actually from Rome during his final imprisonment, that he wrote to the faithful congregation at Colossae (a small township in what is now Turkey) warning them against being led astray from the hard, historic fact of the Incarnation by "false teachers", namely Judaizers, human-centred philosophers, mystics and such like. He emphasizes the pre-eminence of Christ, his supremacy, his all-sufficiency. He writes:

> See to it that no one takes you captive through philosophy and empty deceit according to human tradition, according to the elemental spirits of the universe, and not according to Christ (Col 2.8).

He appealed to their understanding to grasp the finality of Christ:

> He is the image of the invisible God, the first-born of all creation, for in him all things in heaven and earth were made, things visible and invisible, whether thrones or dominions, or rulers or powers - all things have been created through him and for him. He himself is before all things, and in him all things hold together. He is the head of the body, the church; he is the beginning, the first-born from the dead so that he might come to have first place in everything (Col 1.15 -18).

The discerning reader will notice how close St. Paul's thinking is to St. John's when he comes to explaining the Incarnation.

We began this chapter with the question Christ put to his disciples. "And what about you yourselves? Who do you say that I am?" Let us keep this question in mind as we study in the following pages: how the disciples grew in their spiritual understanding from Jesus to Christ; how the New Testament theologians explained it; and finally how modern men and women may apprehend and comprehend the meaning of that unique divine event.

There is one further difficulty and difference inherent in Christianity compared with its two kindred biblical faiths, Judaism and Islam (apart from the difficulty of adequate language mentioned above). A devout and devoted Jew can exercise his faith to the full in his devotion to Judaism and live a full and good life in any society and settle all his failings at the annual Festival of the Atonement, and renew himself for a fresh start. By contrast, a Muslim, in his devotion to Islam, is more at home in an Islamic, theocratic state. But in the case of a Christian, he knows deep down that there has been only one true "Christian," only one true human being, the Last Adam, Jesus himself, and at his best, the faithful believer knows that he does not have the faith of Christ, but is in process of becoming Christian. This can mean that others see us as hypocrites paying homage to virtue; and critics - Jewish, Muslim, secular alike - see our theology as unacceptable hypocrisy. We may admit they have a point, but one may positively assert that we offer to all mankind, Jesus the Christ, the perfect, divine expression of and for all humankind. We sum up all things in Christ, we disclose the divine "mystery of Christ." We preach not ourselves, not our religion, but Christ, the Light of the world (2 Cor 4.5-6; Jn 8.12-14). "For we do not proclaim ourselves; we proclaim Jesus Christ as Lord" (2 Cor 4.5).

Christ put this fact of birth from above to Nicodemus, the finest example of Judaism in the New Testament (John 3),[13] though of course not in 21st-century terms, but in the thought forms of his day. If Nicodemus cannot understand earthly truths (επιγεια), how can he understand divine truths (επιροντα)? To the master of Israel, this question exposed the full truth of the Incarnation. If he had answered this question, the whole truth of Christ would have been his. That is why St. John put this incident at the beginning of his Gospel.

What do we learn from this incident? Answer: the only way is to receive from God a new mind, by grace alone (χαρις), for we cannot raise and find answers about knowing God from any position outside that realm, certainly not from our normal human level. The question can only be understood at that level and in its own terms. And this is precisely what Christ is there for.

This is exactly what Paul teaches in Ephesians, when he argues that such matters are only understood by reason *and* revelation (Eph 1.17),

---

[13] Nicodemus, a senior rabbi and a secret disciple of Jesus, receives fuller treatment on p. 115.

i.e. by the rational mind as it discerns truth (a faculty we all have) *together* with the spiritual insight, graciously and freely offered by God in Christ, offered to the humble and penitent heart.

What Christ presents in the Incarnation is the manifestation in the flesh of humanity, perfect and complete: he is the Last Adam. As such, in his perfect obedience to the will of God, his Father, he expresses God's will for all humanity, i.e. he expresses the mind of God to us men and women. Jesus Christ created and creates a new humanity. "As all die in Adam, so all will be made alive in Christ" (1 Cor 15.22). By "one man" (Adam), St. Paul is saying, sin and death entered into the world; so also by one man (Christ) righteousness and new life have now entered into the world. The original intention of God in the creation, frustrated by Adam's disobedience, is now capable of fulfilment through the restoration achieved by Christ. "If anyone is in Christ, there is a new creation" (2 Cor 5.17; cf. Gal 6.15).

We now turn to an account of how the ordinary folk and the disciples gradually began to understand that Jesus was the Christ.

2

From Jesus to Christ

a. *The Authority of Jesus*

In this chapter we shall study those occasions in the Synoptic Gospels when, in his preaching ministry, Jesus was questioned on the nature of his authority, but more important, those "supernatural" events where his nature and being were revealed and disclosed. Those special occasions were: the Nativity stories, the Baptism, the Temptation, his private teaching of the disciples, Peter's confession at Caesarea Philippi, the Transfiguration, the Resurrection and the Ascension. How the theologians of the New Testament, John the Evangelist, Paul and the author of the Epistle to the Hebrews, interpreted these events, we leave to Part II.

It is perfectly clear from the Gospel writers, and from the views of the common folk who "heard him gladly," that Jesus was thoroughly a normal human being. He is clearly portrayed as a first-century Jew undergoing all the normal human and emotional reactions and experiences common to man. He was born and underwent all the experiences of childhood to manhood. He calls himself a man (Jn 8.40) and speaks of his body and its impending dissolution, of its reality after his resurrection (Lk. 24.6-7). He is described as experiencing all the human emotions: compassion, love of friends, agony, tears, thirst, weariness, sleep, death.

Yet it is equally clear that the common people began to ask who this person was. A prophet? Or more than a prophet? As for the disciples, they began to realize an authority about him, mysteriously compelling, in the miracles he performed, and in his claim to forgive sins. He claimed a special relationship with God, whom he called his Father, and himself his Son (Mt 11.25-27). All these claims were vindicated in the Resurrection. They grew in their understanding of Jesus to seeing him as a Christ, as God's own Messiah to redeem the world. All this thinking was developed by St. John, St. Paul, and the author of Hebrews (see Part II).

The impression given on reading the Synoptic Gospels is that Jesus seems reticent about disclosing his nature and even his authority. He claimed an authority even over the Mosaic Law: "You have heard that it was said to those of ancient times ... But I say unto you ..." (Mt 5.21, 27, 31, 35, 38, 43). True, he used such titles as Son of Man, and Son of God, but these titles had long been used in the history of the Jews, and with wide connotations. They did not mean Christ, the Messiah, specifically.

But this lack of precision and exactness is easily and naturally explained. In the first place, he did not want to be understood in the generally accepted terms of a conquering Messiah who would rid his people of the enemy and restore to them their Promised Land. His messiahship was *sui generis*. His kingdom was not of this world but of God, a spiritual kingdom for all, where men, women, and children would dwell in love, joy, peace, and fellowship one with another. Further, and a more important reason, it was essential to his purpose (and always will be and always is) that people should *perceive* this of and by themselves and not merely be *told* this and accept it. Religious truth has to be perceived and believed to be true before it is fully and truly apprehended.

A similar interpretation of Christ's reticence to declare his own nature but to demand of his questioners the requirement that they should perceive this of themselves, is given to his questioners on his final visit to Jerusalem when the chief priests, the scribes and elders finally asked him, "By what authority are you doing these things, and who gave you this authority to do them?" (Mk 11.28). He had just driven out of the Temple those who sold and bought there, the moneychangers, and those who were making the Temple a market place, saying, "The Temple is a house of prayer for all nations." Jesus turned their question to themselves, "I will ask you a question; answer me, and I will tell you by what authority I do these things. Was the baptism of John from heaven or from men?" They evaded the question, saying they did not know. Jesus replied, "Neither will I tell you by what authority I do these things." It was as John's: divine authority.

b. *The Nativity Stories*

The Nativity narratives teem with indications and prognostications that this birth was the birth of the promised Messiah. I am not discussing the naked historicity of these events, but merely drawing out their meaning, and what the Evangelists intended us to understand of Christ in these stories. They are writing about the beginnings of the greatest event in all history for all mankind for all time, to those people at that time, in the only way people of that time could or would understand.

The writers are telling us that this unique birth of Christ was not the fruit of any culture, nor the natural result of any marriage, but the creation of God himself in fulfilment of his promise to Abraham. Mary was told in advance by an angel from heaven that she was to give birth to the Son of God, and that his kingdom would last for ever. Her cousin Elizabeth was informed similarly that, though past childbearing (to emphasize that it was all effected by God) she was to give birth to a great prophet destined to prepare the way for Christ, to bring salvation and peace to humankind. The common shepherds were told by the angels from heaven of the good news of Christ the Lord for all man-kind, and the Wise Men of the World came from the far corners of the earth to pay homage to Christ. All these details in unforgettable words speak of God's love and concern for lost mankind and of his Son whom he was sending to save people from their sin and error and in-troduce the Kingdom of God for all people. Does not the sheer poetry of it all lighten the mind and warm the heart in a way prose cannot? It is an invitation to see and understand. As William Blake expressed it:

> This life's dim windows of the soul
> Distort the heavens from pole to pole
> And lead you to believe a lie
> When you see with not through the eye.

Of course belief in the Incarnation does not depend on these stories, but on the facts of the life of Jesus, his words and his deeds, and how those who saw and heard those deeds and words, and believed them, recorded and interpreted them for all time, for all men, to create faith in Christ in all humankind. Nevertheless, when the nature of Christ is discussed, his mission, message and ministry, there always creeps in a kind of super-charged language carrying a deeper and more profound meaning. This is as it should be, for when you are thinking of God, or Christ, or the nature and destiny of man, what is required is language and thought above and beyond our normal everyday language. It may not be the exalted, heavenly language of the Nativity stories where even heaven speaks, nay sings, and shines in divine light, nor even the divine language of prophet, psalmist, saint, but it must be your own language raised to an epistemological level which can cope with God, Christ, the gospel, and understand their meaning. Otherwise, you will never believe, never understand. If we include the genealogical tables of Matthew and Luke (Mt 1.1-17; Lk 3.23-34) with the Nativity stories, it is noteworthy for the present study that Jesus is referred to as the Christ.

But before we examine those specific debates on Christ's nature, I would like to take a closer look at the very familiar Nativity stories, not to use them as any authority, but to invite the reader to understand them at a higher level of poetic truth, of spiritual insight, as I have argued on the reason Jesus taught in parables. In other words, what did Matthew and Luke *intend* in their stories, what meaning of the Christ event were they seeking to tell the world?

Matthew tells the story of an angel of the Lord visiting Joseph of the lineage of David, informing him of the unique and impossible birth of a son to his virgin betrothed Mary, and as God explained to him in a dream, to treat Mary honourably, for this son must be called Jesus, the Saviour. Matthew then goes on to tell the story of the Wise Men of the World, who by divine guidance, visited the Holy Family on the birth of Jesus, bringing gifts of gold (for a king), frankincense (to worship God), and strangely myrrh (the death it would cost a saviour of this world). And how it was this world (represented by Herod) would seek the destruction of Jesus. But also, how the Holy Family and the Wise Men outwitted Herod (again under divine guidance), though he wrought vengeance in the massacre of all babies of that age.

As you consider this story, remember also Luke's account, bearing in mind he was a cultivated man who accompanied Paul on his missionary journeys, and who expressly declared he was writing a true historical account "after investigating everything carefully from the very first."

He begins with the story of Zechariah the priest (with his genealogy) and his wife Elizabeth (with genealogy), distressed at having no children, who in their old age were promised by a visiting angel (Gabriel, sent by God), that Elizabeth was to give birth to a son, to be named John (the Baptist), who was destined to prepare the way for Jesus Christ. And for five months she hid herself in her own home.

The next month, the sixth (all recorded by Luke the physician), the same angel, Gabriel, was sent by God to a virgin, Mary, not yet married, at that time engaged, to Joseph, of the line of David. She was not to be afraid, for it was God's work for her to be the mother of this child, who was to be the Son of God, whose kingdom would have no end. Gabriel also gave her the news that her cousin Elizabeth was already six months pregnant (with John the Baptist) who, as Elizabeth expressed it, "leaped for joy in her womb" at the news. And Mary remained with Elizabeth "for about three months."

Luke goes on to say that all these things were talked about through-out the hill country of Judea.

Luke then proceeds to tell the story of the birth of John the Baptist and the birth of Jesus, the latter with the story of the angels telling the good news to the shepherds that the Christ was born in Bethlehem, as promised in the Scriptures, and that this good news of the gospel was for all humanity. The shepherds found the babe lying in a manger. The whole story is told and accompanied by the most beautiful poetry that eventually found its way into the Book of Common Prayer for daily use. Luke completes his story with an account of Jesus' circumcision and presentation in the Temple, his strong and vigorous boyhood, and finally at the age of twelve (now an adult), sitting among the theologi-ans in the Temple and asking them questions.

These stories recount in beautiful poetic language that God prepared the way in his own good time and in his own way, the coming of Jesus. Jesus was born, not of a man's will, nor of any normal sexual desire, but wholly of God and to fulfil his own purpose. The stories recount all this, and of the universe singing for joy at the love and grace of God, for the message was meant for all humanity, the whole world; of the intellectuals of the wide earth perceiving they had reached their jour-ney's end in Christ; of the evil men who would always seek to destroy him. All this and much more conveyed in stories that little children receive and understand in silent wide-eyed awe.

I "prove" nothing from these stories. To a generation that is blinded in its devotion to the *ignis fatuus*[1] of "literal truth," I suggest we elevate our minds to the levels of truth the artist sees, the poet sees, the child sees, and in those levels see and perceive, hear and understand. As Lu-ther simply said:

> When you have laid hold of Christ as man,
> that will soon bring with it the knowledge
> of him as God. (WA V, 129, 9-11)

But all that is rather by way of introduction. We turn now to the is-sues and questions raised by Christ's own contemporaries as well as modern man on his nature, being, and mission, recounted in the Syn-optic Gospels (Matthew, Mark and Luke).

At the least, these stories do attempt to handle mighty and eternal themes: God's love and concern for wayward, sinful man; the child of eternity to be the Eternal Christ; the origin and nature of Christ, the

---

[1] A deceiving light, a "will-of-the-wisp."

cosmic, eternal universal Christ, at whose coming heaven and earth rang out with joy; Christ the light of the universe; Christ the hope of all the world; Christ, God's Idea for all mankind. With respect to our clergy, I never hear these mighty themes from the pulpit nowadays. I reflect on the great Christmas sermons of the past, of Luther and Calvin, the Englishman Lancelot Andrews, and the mighty heartening themes of the Christmas story. On a recent Christmas day at a church I had to listen to the vicar singing from the pulpit, to the strumming of his guitar, modern Christmas songs about bells and reindeer, while the church warden doled out mince pies to the congregation. This is not our Christmas message. Why can't we hear about the Incarnation, what it is, and what it means? At least the Nativity stories tell us.

c. *The Baptism of Jesus*

The Baptism of Jesus (Mt 3.15-17; Mk 1.9-11; Lk 3.21-22), proclaimed the first declaration of the messiahship of Jesus. It was heralded by the mission of John the Baptist, which was foretold in the Nativity stories. John came preaching a mission of national repentance, when multitudes followed him, including Pharisees and Sadducees, to be baptized in the River Jordan. Among the multitudes stood Jesus. In his messianic preaching, John declared that there was one standing among them, prophesied by Isaiah, who would baptize with the Holy Spirit and with fire, in contrast to his baptism with mere water. Jesus presented himself. John demurred at Jesus offering himself, saying that he should be submitting himself to Jesus. Jesus insisted, for he identified himself with the people completely. What is at issue is the Incarnation. The crowds averred that at that moment they were aware of the Holy Spirit alighting on Jesus as gently as a dove, and that they heard a voice from heaven, saying, "This is my beloved Son, in whom I am well pleased" (Mt 3.17).

Whatever the modern reader makes of this incident, he/she should consider what meaning the Evangelists are conveying. They are saying, in the only vocabulary they possessed, that this historic incident of physical baptism in the River Jordan was graced by the presence of the Holy Spirit and by confirmation of God's word, that this Jesus, standing among them, was the promised Messiah of God. It was not a matter of what many people thought about Jesus, or what the religious authorities thought about him. It was what God declared him to be. Whatever the reader makes of the incident, let him/her grasp what the Evangelists are saying.

The importance of this event is its messianic significance. It is in a sense the "coronation" of Jesus as the Messiah, his public installation. The Father confirms his public identity. He confers his Holy Spirit. This anointing furnishes him with the spiritual endowment requisite for the fulfilment of his messiahship. In the strength of this nourishment he faced the Temptation of "Satan" forty days and forty nights. To that we now turn.

d. *The Temptation of Jesus* (Mt 4.1-11; Mk 1.12-13; Lk 4.1-13)
The biblical idea of temptation is not primarily of seduction, as in modern usage, but of making trial of a person, or putting him to the test. This may be done in two ways: positively, with the benevolent intent of providing or improving his quality so that he emerges a finer man after his ordeal; or negatively, with the malicious aim of trapping him in his weakness and so destroy his character.

The first way, the positive way, God's way, is exemplified in the Old Testament where God tests his people to see (or rather show) whether his people are faithful to their covenant with him (Deut 8.2, 16; 13.3). It is significant that it is Israel, never the heathen, he puts on trial. These are tests of obedience and of faith. It is those whom he has called who are tested. We see this clearly in the call of Abraham and in the severest of tests, to sacrifice his son, Isaac, his only son, born in his old age, and on whom, humanly speaking, lay the solitary hope of the promise. It was against all common sense, all common humanity. On Abraham's faith rested even the birth of Christ. On such faith the redemption of mankind depends. God brings those he most values into testing situations, as in the story of Job, to refine obedience and strengthen faith. The Psalms teem with such situations.

The second way, the negative way, is the way of the "Tempter," "Satan" the "enemy."[2] We are compelled in this context to personalize this force of evil, because the power attacks us at the personal level. It is always an assault on personal faith. Its purpose is to destroy our faith and obedience and provoke us to unfaith, to rebellion against God.

Yet, under God, these negative, evil assaults can be defeated. As Calvin expressed it, *Il faut que Dieu gagne* (God will prevail).

A perfect scriptural example can be given in St. Paul's writings. In 2 Cor 12, Paul reluctantly tells the story of how he was once caught up into the third heaven (i.e. God's presence), into paradise, where he

---

[2] If I may be permitted to use the biblical terminology in this context and not enter a critical study of the words and ideas. The biblical personification does convey the objective nature of these attackers as they attack the person in real life.

learned things no man may "utter." Of this abundance of revelations he could boast, but he will only speak of his weaknesses. And to prevent his being too elated by this experience of God, God gave him "the thorn in the flesh, a messenger from Satan, to harass me, to prevent me from being too elated." That was so that Paul would learn the lesson that:

> My grace is sufficient for you,
> For my power is made perfect in weakness.

Paul went on to say:

> I will boast all the more gladly of my weaknesses, so that the power of Christ may dwell in me. Therefore I am content with weaknesses, insults, hardships, persecutions and calamities for the sake of Christ. For, whenever I am weak, then I am strong.

This is the perfect transmutation of an evil assault from Satan, permitted by God, so that Paul would learn the sufficiency of grace, that is, the power of Christ in one's mind and heart.

Jesus himself was tested by Satan at the very outset of his ministry and subtly tempted to abandon God's way of redemption, and as a powerful preacher, a miracle worker, and leader of the people, strike when the iron was hot, and inaugurate immediate, effective action which the common people would immediately understand and cooperate to set out on his own programme of messianic conquest, effective by power rather than by suffering. Who wants that way, anyhow? Christ called Satan "a murderer and a liar from the beginning," i.e. at the outset of humanity's story in the Garden of Eden. By murder, Christ means the destruction of our life, and by "liar" he means that all Satan's ideas and ways are false and not true. "He does not stand in the truth, because there is no truth in him" (Jn 8.44).

And here emerges the significance of the Temptation for our present enquiry. Each of the three temptations is preceded by the words, "*If you are the Son of God* ...." It was precisely for this reason he was in the wilderness, namely to find out from God what messiahship God intended for Jesus in his role as the Son of God, the Messiah. The Devil sought to change Jesus' mind by quoting the Scriptures' divine authority.[3] Christ refuted such self-indulgent exegesis each time by true exegesis. Satan was seeking to destroy Christ's own relationship to God, and God's inherent righteousness, but primarily his messiahship. All this at the outset of his ministry when he was wrestling with God on God's

---

[3] Shakespeare noted this: "The devil can cite Scripture for his purpose" (*Merchant of Venice*, III, ii, 99).

intention for his messiahship. He endured temptation indirectly from the Pharisees and doctors of the law all his life (Mk 8.11; 10.3 etc.).

This he endured until Gethsemane, when after the deepest conflict he rose to face traitor, High Priest, Pilate, and the cross, with that immortal "Nevertheless ..." on his lips. He neither faltered nor failed, but the conviction that he was God's Messiah at the cost of the Cross, first forged at the Temptation, remained with him to the end.

We should always remember that all this detail about the Temptation could have come only from Jesus himself and was not invented by the Evangelists, for it is expressly stated that he was alone in the wilderness, unaccompanied by any disciple. No doubt this was on one of those occasions when "privately to his disciples he explained everything" (Mk 4.10).

In Mk 4.10 it is recorded that when he was alone, his disciples came to him and asked why he taught in parables, and he answered (v. 11):

> To you has been given the secret of the Kingdom of God
> But to those outside everything is in parables.

In this context he quotes the prophet Isaiah (Isa 6.9-10):

> They shall indeed look, but not perceive,
> and may indeed listen, but not understand.

He later says, privately, to his own disciples, "he explained everything" (Mk 4.34). That was all the authority the disciples needed - and we disciples, too.

It may be appropriate at this juncture to say that there follow periods of itinerant preaching, as well as preaching in the synagogues, based on the prophetic teaching of his messiahship when they all wondered where he got such wisdom (Mk 6.2), and at Nazareth, where he had been brought up. When he preached his first sermon and exposition of Isaiah 61, they all wondered at the gracious words which fell from his lips (Lk 4.22 and parallels). "Where did this man get all this?" As they expressed it, he drove out the demons from those possessed and the demons on being driven out cried out that he was "the Holy One of God" (Mk 1.24). It was the belief at that time that the demons had a supernatural existence and therefore recognized the super-human power of Christ. (Modern medical knowledge would of course express the disorder in modern terms, though not the power in Christ. The issue here is the revelation of the messianic authority in Jesus.)

In recording Jesus' ministry of preaching, teaching and healing, Mark speaks of Jesus as "preaching the word" in a house in Capernaum (Peter's house?) (Mk 2.2ff.). ("Preaching the word" was everything he had to say about God's purposes.) He is interrupted by some men who actually tear a hole in the roof and lower a paralytic friend at the feet of Jesus as he is preaching. Touched by such ardent faith in him, he addresses the sick man with an affectionate word, he heals him and forgives him his sins,[4] presumably to wipe away his wrong past (probably well-known to Jesus), and in restoring him, grant him a new start.

The scribes "sitting there" accuse Jesus of blasphemy, for only God can forgive sin. It is in this context he tells the hostile scribes that the purpose of his action is "that they may know" he is the Son of Man (Mk 2.10) – a clear declaration of his nature as the Christ.

e. *The Confession of Peter at Caesarea Philippi*
(Mt 16.13-23; Mk 8.27-33; Lk 9.18-22)

The complete answer on Christ's own interpretation of himself is found in the confession at Caesarea Philippi when Jesus asked his disciples, "Who do people say that I am? ... Who do you say that I am?" Peter answered, "You are the Christ." And he ordered them not to tell anyone. Again, for the reason given above, that people must perceive this of themselves and experience the entire change in their whole ontological being. That change creates understanding. The enquirer no longer stands "without"; he/she becomes a believer, a disciple standing within the Kingdom. He must perceive this by himself and appropriate it for himself; he learns little or nothing if he is merely told it.

The story is highly significant for the present study. It was the first time that the disciples had formulated their belief in Christ. Further, the story is closely linked with the episode that follows, the Transfiguration, precisely dated in Matthew and Luke as six days later (see below, p. 39). The significance of the story is seen in a close study of the Markan text. No stress is laid on Peter's confession as such, as in Matthew's account. He makes a confession which any disciple, even every believer makes about Jesus - even the demons saw that (2.24, 34; 3.11; 5.7). The remarkable thing is that the disciples are rebuked (as were the demons), censured. The real heart of the matter is that Jesus immediately warned them that he must go to Jerusalem, would be rejected by the priests,

---

[4] The current belief of Judaism was that disease was a result of sin. That was the sick man's view and Jesus spoke to his condition. As it was in Capernaum, Jesus may well have known the man, for he addressed him with an affectionate term. Of course, Jesus may well have discerned his trouble. We might well explain it all in different terms today, but we must not overlook that fact that much disease, though not all, is a result of wrong and sinful living e.g. alcohol abuse, smoking, gluttony, sexual licence, etc.

the elders and the scribes, suffer death but rise again after three days. And Mark adds that Jesus spoke openly of this way of the cross, while his real nature as the Messiah, which the disciples had perceived, was secret to themselves.

Here is portrayed the difference between the purely Judaic and Christ's awareness of his messiahship. The messiahship is from now on only to be viewed in the light of the cross (the stumbling block to the Jews, foolishness to the Greeks, 1 Cor 1.23). In fact, the whole tone of Mark's Gospel changes at this point. All teaching is from now on about the cross.[5] The doctrine of messiahship, apart from the cross, could only be misleading. That is why Christ rebuked the disciples. They were not to make him known in such terms. The doctrine of the Son of Man (with its corollary, the Way of the Cross, for the true disciple) was the very gospel which was to be proclaimed to all the world, and therefore, as Mark clearly states, Jesus "spoke the saying openly" (Mk 8.32). And, to make it more emphatic, when Peter had the temerity to rebuke Jesus for such uncompromising teaching, Jesus rebuked him as talking like Satan, for setting his mind "not on divine things but on human things" (v. 33).[6]

Christ is most emphatic here on the nature of true discipleship, disciple and multitude alike:

> He called the crowd with his disciples and said to them: If any want to become my followers, let them deny themselves and take up their cross and follow me.
>
> For those who want to save their life will lose it, and those who lose their life for my sake and for the sake of the Gospel will save it.
>
> For what will it profit them to gain the whole world and forfeit their life? Indeed, what can they give in return for their life? (Mk 8.35-37)

No price can deliver or buy back from death a life, a soul, which in a deeper sense is "lost." As Kierkegaard expressed it: "The question is whether the New Testament recognizes any kind of Christian other than 'the disciple'."[7]

A rather touching and revealing incident is when John the Baptist, now in prison for his criticism of Herod, sends some of his disciples to ask Jesus whether after all he was right in his prophecy of Jesus as the

---

[5] T.W. Manson argued this in his enduring book *The Teaching of Jesus*, 1931.

[6] Luther rebuked Erasmus in these very words, after reading Erasmus, "On Free Will," 1525.

[7] *Journals of Kierkegaard* (Fontana, 1958), p. 228.

Messiah. Jesus asks John's disciples to go back to John and report what they themselves now see and hear:

> The blind receive their sight, the lame walk, the lepers are cleansed and the deaf hear, the dead are raised, and the poor have the good news brought to them. And blessed is anyone who takes no offence at me.   (Mt 11.4-6)

The evidence is self-evident. They were to see for themselves that Jesus had fulfilled John's prophecy that he was the Messiah. And this is precisely what anybody who seeks to understand Christ must learn.

And then there are those two fearful and perturbing incidents of Jesus calmly stilling the storm (Mt 8.18ff.; Mk 4.35ff.; Lk 8.22ff.), and of walking on the waters of Galilee to reach his endangered disciples (Mt 14.23-33; Mk 6.45-52). Whatever modern people may make of these stories, the people who were there interpreted them as natural to Christ, and the disciples who experience these strange and terrifying events say to Christ, "Truly, you are the Son of God" (Mt 14.33).

At the risk of repetition, let me express this life-giving truth in other words. Only God in Christ can make you understand who you are. God does not demand of you blind faith, but a *deeper understanding*. Whatever you make of these narratives involving the supernatural, seek primarily to find the meaning the writers were seeking to convey in the only vocabulary and style they had. You will then begin to understand Christ, who he is, and that he came to save you from your own sin and error, and make of you a new creation by the power of his Holy Spirit, which he leaves with you once you understand (or are converted).

Such an understanding of Christ's messiahship is the heart of the gospel, but it is vital to see that it is only God and God alone that will give you this insight, only God can hand you "the candle of understanding."

f. *The Transfiguration*
(Mt 17.1-8; Mk 9.2-8; Lk 9.28-36)
According to the Evangelists, the Transfiguration is closely related in place and date with the Confession at Caesarea Philippi, that Jesus was the Christ, for it shows the glory of Christ and clearly emphasizes his messiahship as superseding both Moses and the prophets. Its deepest significance lies in the fact that, like the Baptism, the disciples heard the authoritative voice of God saying, "This is my beloved Son. Listen to him!" (Mk 9.7).

Many scholars, and most ordinary readers, regard the account as a visionary hallucination, but that brings us no nearer to understanding its meaning and significance. All three Synoptic Gospels place the account at the climax of Jesus' ministry, and God's confirmation of the messiahship of his Son. They all portray the story as the turning point when "he set his face towards Jerusalem." We may not discount or disregard such weighty testimony because it lies outside our experience, or beyond our understanding.

God speaks to the souls of men/women, when he does speak to them, not in divine language (for we humans could neither hear it nor understand it), but in our common ordinary language of seeing and hearing, in such language and imagery as the recipients of his revelation may best be able to understand. Such speech may come through poetry, music, art, our conscience, even on the lips of a good friend or loved one; worse, on the bleak unfolding of the fruits of our own sin and error and misjudgments. It need not necessarily be of a supernatural nature. It is God who speaks; but the criterion of revelation is not in its form, nor does psychological abnormality or strangeness, or eeriness or coincidence guarantee a supposed revelation as being divine. Some mystics are more accustomed to such experiences (the Desert Fathers claimed to have visits from the very Devil).

Any prosaic view or interpretation of the experience leads to the total loss of the supernatural experience of the disciples, an experience all the Synoptists record as the climax of Christ's ministry and the divine proof of Jesus' understanding of his messiahship. Such explanations, therefore, must be regarded as at least misleading. Let us then look at what the Evangelists tell us in an attempt to understand what they are saying and not waste our time on fruitless speculation on the details.

Following close on Peter's confession that Jesus was the Christ, Jesus immediately began to teach the disciples together with the crowds following him the nature of the true discipleship, and this done, took Peter, James and John up a high mountain, where they witnessed Jesus alone in deep, intense prayer with God (Mt 17.1-9; Mk 9.2-10; Lk 9.28-36; cf. 2 Pet 1.16-21). He was transfigured before their eyes. His face shone like the sun, even his garments glistened with a heavenly brightness.

The story of the Transfiguration is of importance to the Evangelists, for it carries (as does the Baptism of Jesus) the direct, supernatural testimony of God himself as to the truth of Christ. Yet, to the modern reader it looks like a fantasy of symbolic writing. It describes how at prayer his countenance was altered, and even his garments glistened in an aura of supernatural light; and how Moses and Elijah appeared and talked with Jesus; how Peter had said it was a good thing they were to witness such an event; and how a cloud (the shekinah, the cloud of God's presence) had overshadowed them, and how, out of the cloud of God's presence, God himself addressed them about Christ, saying, "This is my beloved Son. Listen to him." And suddenly, looking around them they no longer saw anyone with them, only Jesus.

This story had great evidentiary value in the eyes of the Early Church, and still carries weight in the Eastern Orthodox Church, though to most Western minds today it is regarded as myth, even fantasy, and many are the scholars, particularly the liberal German Protestants, who freely assert this. It has the look of some of the apocalyptical writings such as Daniel or Revelation: a kind of symbolic vision. The disciples are now to look on the Law (Moses) and the prophets (Elijah) as superseded and fulfilled in Christ, God's beloved Son; they are to listen to him only.

The pious, prosaic, credulous mind does not meet the present day difficulties, nor does the brutal scientific mind. The matter can only be understood if we put another and different question to the material. What did the writer seek to convey to the reader? What did it all *mean* to him? What *meaning* was in his mind? Could he have expressed such divine transcendental thoughts to such a group in any other way? Could Jesus himself have conveyed to his three inmost disciples, Jews, the meaning of his messiahship in any other way, in any other words? It is perfectly intelligible that a group of Jewish peasants could envisage Moses and Elijah, feel the presence of the Shekinah, should hear the Bath-Qol (God's very voice). They had been brought up to think in terms of Moses and the Law, of Elijah and all the prophets and of the Shekinah, God's actual Presence overshadowing them, and occasionally of the Bath-Qol.

What the modern reader should do is put himself in the mountains with Jesus in deep prayer to his Father, and ask whether it was the Father's will that Jesus as the Messiah was to fulfil his redemptive mission, a mission of tenderness and love, in Jerusalem, on a bloody cross. The three disciples witnessed all this. They perceived the support of Moses (the Law) and of Elijah (Prophecy) convincing them that all this was completed and fulfilled in Jesus now at prayer, and that the power and presence of God had overshadowed them (Shekinah) and brought conviction. The disciples experienced all this, saw and heard and expressed it in their own religious terms. We do not need to ask which mountain it was, Tabor or Shechem. We do not need to ask prosaic questions such as, how would they have recognized Moses and Elijah, whom they had never seen. Such are fruitless speculations. Simply remain agnostic in regard to such details, but reflect deeply and continually on the abiding meaning of the incident. Let it address you.

The narrative clearly shows that Christ's messiahship is the final fulfilment of the work and mission of Moses (the Law) and of Elijah (Prophecy). Each of these had had a vision of the glory of God on a mountain, Moses on Sinai (Ex 24.15) and Elijah on Horeb (1 Kgs 19.8). Each of them has no known grave (Deut 34.6; 2 Kgs 2.11) and each of them is mentioned in the closing verses of the Old Testament (Mal 4.4f.).

The Transfiguration, therefore, is both a climax and focal point in the revelation of the Kingdom of God, for it looks back to the Old Testament dispensation and shows not only that Christ fulfils it, but also looks forward to its completion in the cross, resurrection, ascension and parousia. Even Peter who was there could not understand it, and wanted to mark the event by building three tabernacles to make the event permanent. What was needed was the presence of Jesus alone, and attention to his voice. This kind of language and this way of thinking may not appeal to the modern mind, but the modern mind has the responsibility of seeking to understand how the first-century mind would understand it, for that original understanding is its meaning and it is that meaning which is permanent and it is the meaning we moderns must grasp and understand.

All the issues discussed in this section on the nature and meaning of the messiahship of Jesus were raised again when he finally came to Jerusalem; his lament over the city; his preaching and teaching in the Temple; the questioning of the scribes and Pharisees and Sadducees on his messiahship; his trial before Annas and Caiaphas; his trial before Pilate; and eventually his crucifixion, resurrection and ascension. And so, after the brief summary of how the disciples and apostles saw and gave an account of "these things," more significantly how Christ himself explained his nature and his messiahship, we turn to the resurrection and ascension.

g. *The Resurrection*
(Mt 28; Mk 16; Lk 24)
In the context of our present enquiry where we are studying how the disciples began to believe that Jesus was the Christ, and how they moved from the generally accepted idea of the Messiah to Christ's own explanation of the Messiah God intended, it is noteworthy that in spite

of two explanations of his messiahship, namely at Peter's confession at Caesarea Philippi (Mt 16.14-23; Mk 8.27-33; Lk 9.18-22) and in Galilee (Mt 17.22-23; Mk 9.30-32; Lk 9.42-45), it is recorded that the disciples protested and could neither believe nor understand the resurrection. Even when they saw the empty tomb, all three Evangelists record that the witnesses and the disciples neither understood nor believed, except for John, who saw and believed (Jn 20.8).

There then follow what we call the Appearances. Matthew (ch. 28) tells the story of Mary Magdalene with "the other Mary" going to the tomb early on the Sunday morning to find the tomb empty, and an angel tells them, "He is not here, for he is risen." The angel tells them to break the news to the disciples and then return to Galilee where Christ will meet them. They return to Galilee.

Even there, when the risen Lord appeared, "some doubted." There he gave his final commission:

> All authority in heaven and on earth has been given to me. Go therefore and make disciples of all nations, baptizing them in the name of the Father and of the Son and of the Holy Spirit, and teaching them to obey everything that I have commanded you. And remember, I am with you always, to the end of the age. (Mt 28.18-20)

Mark (ch. 16) tells the same story of the two women going to the tomb early on the Sunday morning, to find the angel who told them that the tomb was empty, Christ was not there for he had risen, and that they were to return home to Galilee, where they would see him, as he promised.

And there Mark ends abruptly. Scholars, on a close study of the early manuscripts and evidence of the Church Fathers, have come to the conclusion that the original closing verses are lost, and that the ending which we read in the Bible comprises two early endings. In this longer ending of Mark, there is narrated Our Lord's appearance to Mary Magdalene, to two disciples out walking (Luke's Emmaus?), and to the eleven disciples at table, whom he upbraided for their unbelief, yet gave them their commission as in Matthew. After speaking to them the Lord was taken up into heaven, and the disciples went forth to preach the gospel, and the Lord "worked with them" in their ministry.

Luke (ch. 24) gives the familiar account of the risen Lord joining two followers as they were walking home on the road to Emmaus on the very day of the resurrection, as they were discussing the strange events of the day. How the risen Christ joined them and opened up to them the meaning of these events from the scriptures, but how slow they were to come to belief. At table, they recognized their guest as he broke the bread, and then he vanished. Their hearts "burned within them," and within the hour, late at night though it was, they returned to Jerusalem to tell the eleven of their amazing experiences.

Luke further tells the story of the appearance of the risen Christ in Jerusalem to his disciples still questioning the meaning of recent events. Christ reassures them it is he himself and no ghost, and he shares a little broiled fish with them. He commissions them to preach the gospel "to all nations" promising them the presence of the Holy Spirit in their ministry. And then Luke adds he led them out to Bethany, blessed them, and in blessing, "parted from them" (the ascension).

In St. John's Gospel (ch. 20) we again read of Mary Magdalene early on the Sunday morning coming to the tomb to find it empty. She rushes away to tell the startling news to Peter and John, who immediately go to see for themselves. There are recorded the pregnant words about John, "He saw and believed." John was the first to believe that the Lord had left the grave clothes behind, had broken away from his earthly life, and was risen – and further, be it said, the first in a long list of blessed disciples who believed without having actually seen the risen Lord. The two disciples went home, but Mary stayed weeping. Through her tears she saw an angelic messenger who asked her why she was weeping. Through the same tears she turned to see a figure behind her, who asked her why she was weeping. He uttered one word, "Mary." It was the voice of the risen Lord. It was not to the beloved disciple, nor to Peter, that he first appeared but to Mary who had stood by the cross on Friday.

We read of the unbelief of Thomas (disbelief is almost a permanent theme in the Resurrection stories), but also of his later conversion and the belief of the Christians. The Gospel account ends, not with the Appearances, but with the commission to the world undertaken by his command and under his authority.

The Fourth Gospel concludes with a remarkable epilogue (ch. 21) almost certainly written by John. It consists of Christ's appearance at Lake Galilee when he guides the disciples in their fruitless fishing to a remarkable catch of 153 fish, after which Peter's fate is discussed as shepherd and martyr, and the destiny of the beloved disciple as the disciple who would never die (a legend which lived on where pilgrims who visited his tomb in Ephesus averred they could hear him breathing if they listened carefully!).

The story teems with symbolism. We cannot go into detail in this study. Why the detail of 153 fish? People of a mathematical turn of mind discern that the number is of mathematical significance.

Now, 153 is the sum of the first natural numbers 1 ... 17. Further, if you were to take the numbers 1 to 17, and consider each number one unit or dot, you would end up with a perfect equilateral triangle with a base line of 17 dots. It is a triangular number. Moreover, 17 is a prime number of the form $2^n + 1$, a term of great interest to mathematicians. Further, Greek biologists believed that in all there were 153 species of fish in the sea.

Whatever the modern reader makes of such comments, one thing is translucent. The eternal Christ meant the gospel had to be preached to all mankind and that he would be with all believers to the end of the world. Such is a fitting conclusion to an account of how the disciples grew from a faith in Jesus to a belief in the cosmic eternal Christ, and that was what they had to tell the world.

h. *The Ascension*

Of necessity, the "ascension" or "exaltation" of Christ is the final disclosure of his nature and being, and conveys a profound revelation. Yet, it is recorded only by Luke, very briefly in Lk 24.51, and in Acts 1.9 with more detail. Its importance in the preaching of the Early Church is testified throughout the New Testament, where it is expressed by a number of terms: to take up (Acts 1.2, 11; 1 Tim 3.16); to exalt (Acts 2.33; 5.31); to sit down at the right hand of God (Eph 1.20; Heb 1.3; 10.12); to go up or ascend (Acts 2.34; Jn 3.12-14; 6.62; 20.7; Eph 4.8-10). Naturally, the Apostles could think only in terms of the prevalent Ptolemaic cosmology, and they thought of Jesus as going "up" (the only term available) to a place beyond the sky called heaven, from whence he would one day return. But the modern reader will readily see that their belief meant much more than the mere words. The phrase "seated at the right hand of God" does not refer to a place at all but to a state of being, a participation with God in his sovereignty over all things, all people. The exalted Jesus had entered a state of being and activity that transcended the limitations of space utterly and completely and altogether. The exalted Jesus had returned to where he was before, at the right hand of God; with God, as co-equal with God. This is the ultimate understanding of Jesus: Christ eternal and universal. It is to fully understand Jesus as the Christ.

At this point I would suggest that Jesus was perfectly aware, even at the beginning of his ministry, that he was sent from God and by God, and that when his work was accomplished he would return whence he came. There are a few adumbrations of this in the Gospels, but there is a striking saying in his sermon at the synagogue in Capernaum recorded in John 6 after the miracle of the feeding of the five thousand.

John records Jesus as saying in his sermon that their forefathers had eaten the manna in the wilderness but were all dead, but that he was the living bread sent by God, and that a man who ate this bread would live forever, and that bread was his body, which he was to give for the life of the world. Some of his disciples (not the Twelve but of his large circle of disciples and followers) demurred at this teaching, but he insisted with his "Very truly ... that unless they ate the flesh of the Son of Man and drank his blood, they would have no life at all"; to eat of his body and drink of his blood is to have eternal life. This he explained as meaning that the believer dwells in him and he in the believer (v. 56). When Jesus saw that some of his disciples could not believe this because they could not understand this, he said that if that were too much for them, "Then what if you were to see the Son of Man ascending to where he was before?" (v. 62). This means that he came from heaven, from God, and it would be to heaven he would return when his ministry was accomplished. And then he adds that his words are spirit and life, and not about flesh.

The ascension means that the body of Christ is no longer present within our framework of time and space, but belongs to the Son of God who is in eternity. To understand this has a significant bearing on the use of the body of Christ imagery to describe both the church and the eucharist. Augustine and the Reformers were insistent that their language had to be understood in a spiritual way, not as a physical reality. For the Reformers, Calvin in particular, and for their successors, this meant that the medieval doctrines of transubstantiation and the visible church as the body and bride of Christ were not true, nor were they scriptural.

In some passages in the New Testament the resurrection is not sharply distinguished from the ascension as two events (cf. Acts 2.23f.; Rom 8.34; Col 3.1; Phil 2.9; 1 Tim 3.16; Eph 1.20; 1 Pet 3.22). But there is a clear distinction between them in theological meaning. It is one thing to say that God raised him from the dead; another thing to say that he now reigns with God in heaven in sovereignty over heaven and earth (though the two ideas are related and may be understood in like terms).

The significance of the ascension is expressed in John 14-16, in Ephesians and in Hebrews, and is discussed in Part II of the present work. Suffice it here to say that the Ascension brings into being a new relationship between Christ and the believer. The ascended Christ is King, all things are in the final analysis under his sovereignty (cf. Eph 1.20; Phil 2.9-11; Heb 1.3; 1 Pet 3.22; Rev 5.11-13). This we must tell the world. The ascended Christ is our Forerunner, the basis of humanity's ultimate acceptance by God (cf. Jn 14.3; Heb 6.20; 10.19-22; Eph 2.6). The ascended Christ is our eternal Priest, praying for us and all humanity, as one who has experienced temptation, suffering, death (Rom 8.34; Heb 4.14-16; 7.25-26), who paid for our salvation on the cross, a ministry which stands forever for all humanity for it remains with God (Heb 7.23-25; 9.26; 1 Jn 2.1-2; Rev 5.6).

What this all means for the Church is that it is on the ascended Christ that the Church depends for its existence. Its worship is a participation in his eternal priesthood; its work the sanctification of all human lives in his manhood as our pioneer and fore-runner who showed the way to live; and its preaching is to set forth his kingly rule. Quite obviously, such an interpretation and understanding of Christ means that Christ was meant for all mankind.

In Part II we shall see how the theologians of the New Testament, John, Paul and the author of Hebrews interpreted the experiences of Christ just narrated.

Part II
The Incarnation Explained

3
The Incarnation according to St. John

The theme that God's ways are not man's ways, nor his thoughts equivalent to man's thoughts, is translucent throughout the Old Testament, Law, Prophets, Psalms and the Wisdom Literature.

a. *Bridging the Gulf between God and Man*
The later Jewish philosophers and Greek philosophers alike, whether they understood Logos as reason, or as meaning speech or word, were always concerned with Logos (Word) as revealing truth, yet never found it possible to bridge that gap which exists between God and man. How is it possible, by means of human language, the only means we have at our disposal, to bridge that gulf between spirit and matter, the one and the many, the infinite and the finite? There was, and is, only one way: to understand Christ.

John explains the Incarnation in the first few verses of his Gospel, by relating reason and revelation, the Logos and the Word in human form as Jesus Christ.

It was John who first perceived that it was this very problem, of bridging the gulf, which Christ resolved and explained. John saw that the problem which metaphysics could not solve, was resolved in the Incarnation on historical grounds. In other words, in our historic situation, in terms of flesh and blood, God would bridge that gap, the great gulf no man could cross for none other could. The Word became flesh, i.e. in human form; man saw, touched and handled him, heard the Logos express himself in human words all understood. Any knowledge of God must rest, therefore, not on human cerebration, but only on the reality of God's activity in the world he had created, and the world he redeemed in God's own way, not the way man had expected. Expressed in theological terms, in Creation and Incarnation.

There is no other way to know God that makes sense in any convincing, ultimate way. You either have to take up the position expressed by Wittgenstein, "Whereof one cannot speak, thereof one must remain silent," or take the Christian position that we humans cannot speak of God who in his own essence cannot be defined in our own space/time terms, but only in such terms as bring Creation and Incarnation together. Only God can explain man. This was the simple but piercing insight Christ gave John, who starts with Creation (as does Genesis), and explains in the fullness of time, its purpose and end and meaning, by means of the Incarnation, i.e. God's way. Here at once we are related to Eternity, and by the same token, to the creaturely world of our existence which it explains. Here is the place of understanding. Here is the one vital truth all Christian believers must understand. This is the one single truth we must offer to the world in all humility and love. We cannot afford to let liberals, modernists and Ebionites explain away this vital, unique relationship with, and understanding of, God.

John's opening words are, "In the beginning was the Word," obviously relating the story he was about to tell with Genesis and Creation, which means the Word was in a state of being at Creation. It does not mean "was" as in the phrase, "Once upon a time there was ..." This Word was in being already before Creation. In the book of Revelation, Christ the Word of God (Rev 19.13) is represented as claiming pre-existence, the Alpha and Omega, the first and the last, the beginning and the end (22.13). Paul says the same, "he is before all things" (Col 1.17). Further, in the high-priestly prayer of John 17, Christ refers to his presence with God before Creation (17.5). In his preaching he said these remarkable words, "Before Abraham was, I am" (Jn 8.58). If we human beings are to speak of God objectively, therefore, it can only be in the light of God's own interaction with the world he created, and further, within that relationship which he established between his world and himself. We are now in the realm of *epirounia*, "heavenly things" (Jn 3.12), not by means of our own insights, but by God's work and word in the Incarnation. We do not arrive at this insight by our own human thinking but by God's work of grace in Christ. There are no ladders to heaven. Christ "came down" (if I may so express it) or came to our human level of existence to raise us to the aion of the divine, or the realm of God, or the Kingdom of heaven, whichever is more meaningful for you. The great creator makes himself a house of clay.

b. *Seeing the Incarnation from Different Levels*

It often proves helpful in understanding a problem to look at it from a different level, sometimes even using different vocabulary. For example, the moment Faraday thought of magnetism in non-Newtonian terms but as a "field force," he burst into a new field of understanding in relation to a very old problem. The moment Christ declared, "You have heard that it was said to those of ancient times, an eye for an eye, a tooth for a tooth, a life for a life. But I say unto you ...," people realized Christ spoke with an utterly different way of seeing things, i.e. not as slaves to the Law but as those who went further and fulfilled the Law. Christ brought out the intended, ultimate meaning. So it is with the Incarnation. First we need to understand the depths of meaning as the New Testament expresses it, and then re-express those truths in the light of contemporary learning, so that our contemporaries may see and understand. It is the mind of Jesus himself that St. John disclosed.

Let us then look at the New Testament accounts. Here we are at once struck by the different levels at which the Incarnation is expressed.

Consider again the Nativity stories of Matthew or Luke discussed in Chapter 2. Note the different levels at which the nature of the child Jesus is stated. We have the very angels from heaven preparing mankind for the greatest event in history, foretold in history, of the Messiah to be born of God by the virgin Mary; the actual birth in a stable, of all places, thus linking heaven and earth; angels from heaven declare his nature, the purpose of it all, his destiny; shepherds who saw it all and heard it all; mysterious Wise Men, guided by heaven from the ends of the earth, bringing him symbolic, prophetic gifts of gold, frankincense and myrrh; the worldly-wise (Herod) seeing him as a threat and a challenge; and we have the eyes of the artist, the poets, the hymn writers, and even little children, all of whom open our eyes to the depths hidden in these accounts. But, of course, our understanding of the Incarnation relies on Christ's later ministry and teaching, on Apostles such as John and Paul, and on Hebrews. Christ never deployed these Nativity stories as any kind of authority. They spoke for themselves to enlighten sensitive hearts. Christ spoke truth direct to men and women, face to face, for them to see for themselves.

It is to John we first turn.

c. *The Interpretation of St. John's Gospel*

John begins before Creation, exactly as Christ did, "Before Abraham was, I am" (Jn 8.5). A complete understanding of the Incarnation must begin with Creation.

In the beginning was the Word, and the Word was with God. This gives expression to the thought that at Creation the Word already existed, and was already with God. That means already a personal being in fellowship with God and who was God. The Word is no creation, no creatura. He is divine in himself by his own being, as God the Father is. All things were made by him. He is the Agent of the Father, and was to fulfil that mission in re-creating mankind, or as we generally express it, for the redemption of mankind.

In him was life. Life does not exist in the world of physical things. Things do not have life in themselves, but only in, through and by means of the Word, the expression of the Godhead. And this life brought man light, a light never to be put out. The darkness has not, and darkness cannot, overcome light.

The Word became flesh. In other words, the Word became human (the Incarnation) and dwelt among us. The corpus of the disciples will later add that they had all seen these things themselves, and they all testified that John's account was true (Jn 21.24f.). Further, they all beheld "the glory" of the only Son of the Father.

It is well worth reading John's piercing and penetrating account alongside the Nativity stories. He tells us that the child was God. He tells us this after he has seen that child's mission foretold and fulfilled in the man Jesus, before his very eyes, a mission that he shared as a disciple, and recorded for the world.

How are we to understand all this?

Not only does the Word exist before everything, but John uses a more classical Greek form to say more than that the Word was "with God" (the nearest we can get in English translation), but that the Word was (imperfect) and in a continuous process or intention of leading us to God. This is deep insight. Still more, not merely to God, but to *the* God, i.e. the God and Father of our Lord and Saviour, Jesus Christ: God as distinguished from the idea of god hypotheses or god imagined by religious or philosophical humanity. In other words, this Word leads us to the true God. Further, he states uncompromisingly the divinity of the Logos, i.e. the Word was God. He is later to complete his argument by saying that this Word was expressed in human form, in Jesus. This is the staggering claim of Christianity, a claim that

Jew and Muslim reject outright, like contemporary Westerners. Yet, if seen and understood, it explains everything.

John goes on to say (v. 3) that "all things" severally, i.e. as distinct from the Cosmos as a whole, came into being "through the Word." The phrase "all things" signified a new thing, a becoming, a creation, in contrast with the "*being*" of the Word, which was in existence before Creation. He emphasizes (against the Gnostics' belief in the eternity of matter as well as the co-operation of other agencies in Creation), that the one and only agency in Creation was the Word of God.

d. *Different Levels of Awareness*

Apart from the Incarnation, it is readily seen that the natural man may well have a natural knowledge of God, i.e. people know that God exists, opposes evil and favours the good. But all such knowledge is limited to man's human awareness, to human rational understanding, to human language - a very limited awareness indeed. Since Gödel, we have learnt the limitation of human reason in explaining any phenomenon - relativity, quantum mechanics, everything. Amongst other things, he is saying that if anything is to be explained *totally*, there must be at least two levels of interpretation. This is a most valuable insight *in eo ipso*, but in theological thinking it is of extraordinary assistance.

We cannot explain or even understand the rationality of God. Manifestly, it is other than, different from, human rationality. We cannot understand how or why God created the Universe; how God views the Universe or the world he created as it works itself out in time; how he sees humanity's pitiable frustration of his purpose and plan. We have no objective ground on which to stand, no experience to aid us, no language to explain it. Gödel is telling us that it takes several levels of awareness if we are to begin to attempt to explain God and argue his reality. The lesson is to deliver ourselves from the self-imposed bondage to science to explain the mystery of being and to see a larger reality in life than physics, chemistry and mathematics impose. This wholeness Christ offered and still offers. Christ opened John's eyes: let John open ours.

e. *Christ as Explained by John*

The genius of Christianity, and here it is unique among all religions, so perceptively perceived by John, is associating Christ with Creation, Christ with God, time with eternity. John explained this relationship as Jesus' being in the bosom of the Father while walking this earth, limited only in and by obedience to the Father's will for him, while sojourning on this earth to fulfil his Father's will for the redemption of humanity. He said he would return to his Father whence he came, after fulfilling God's will for the redemption of fallen mankind. He promised that mankind would never be left as lost orphans, but that those who believed his Word would have the presence of the Holy Spirit, that God and he would come and live in the hearts and minds of believers. It is in Christ, and only in Christ, that we may experience God to the full – Father, Son and Holy Spirit. It is in Christ, and only in and through Christ, that we experience and understand God. God grants the Holy Spirit as a foretaste to explain our present existence and prepare us for eternity. So Christ explained to John. So John explains to us.

That which has come into being in him was life. This means that the life that was eternally in the Word has issued in created life. This is true both of the physical world and of the spiritual world. Jesus Christ, Son and Word, is the Life (Jn 11.35; 14.6) and the Living One (Rev 1.17), and it is through this Life that all things were created and hold together (Col 1.17). This is equally true of the spiritual life. The Son has life *in himself* (Jn 5.26), and gives life to anyone he wishes to (5.21), i.e. in the sense of purpose, or intent, design. Such are quickened by a spiritual breathing (v. 13). The first movement of this divine word (Gen 1.3) was the creation of light, which created life in the cosmos. As the Psalmist thinks of the Divine Light as the same things, we see that they are: light means life.[1]

As the Life of the World, Jesus raises Lazarus from the dead (Jn 11). As the Light of the World, he gives sight to the blind. We speak not of broad spiritual truths, but of their actual manifestation in the world of events, to known individuals, in known places, at known times, which people saw, even questioning the beneficiaries (12.9). Such are the affective manifestations of the Word of God to all men. And as the light dissipated the darkness of chaos and disorder, so does Christ. Note carefully here in v. 5 the present tense, the light *shines* in the darkness, as Christ does in our present world of darkness and dispute, of decay and death. Christ is the true light that lightens everyone on earth, "true" not in the sense that other lights are false, but "true" in the sense of being final, last, perfect. It is God's word. It is God. As humans we have nothing to add, nothing to say. And finally, note carefully how John has *all mankind* in his sights throughout. Would

---

[1] See Wesley's Christmas hymn, "Hark the Herald Angels Sing": "Light and life to all he brings."

that some godly Jews, some godly Christians, some godly Muslims and others like minded, would get together and think at this level. All our doubts, difficulties, disputes and despair would disappear as the nightly dew disappears before the morning sun. What is certain is that we must raise our thinking out of the rut it has set itself to the level envisioned by John.

From these celestial heights, this divine eloquent language, John turns to the prose of history, reminding us always that though he writes history, its true understanding and meaning is measured in divine language and understanding. But he does not descend to the Nativity stories of angels from heaven and birth in the stable, of shepherds in the fields and wise men from the East, but to the hard, historical fact of John the Baptist in flesh and blood, the promised messenger of the Messiah, who prepared the way for the historical manifestation of the Word, the herald of Christ. Recall at this point that John, our Fourth Evangelist, had first been a disciple of John the Baptist before he became a disciple of Jesus.

The Evangelist states starkly: There arose a man *sent from God* whose name was John. He does not describe him as John the Baptist, but simply as John, for to John (the Evangelist) there was only one John, John the Baptist. His role was a witness, so that all might *believe* through his testimony. John the Baptist was not the Light, rather a lamp. It is as blunt as that. It is noteworthy that John uses the word "to believe" as a verb about one hundred times, never the noun faith, belief, i.e. not as an abstract noun, but as verbal activity.

What this means is that faith is not merely assent or acceptance (*fides*) but total trust (*fiducia*), experienced, found, fulfilled and proven, in the natural doing of following Christ, and living the faith. John was later to emphasize this in his striking phrase of *doing* the truth (not simply knowing it). See Jn 3.20-21; 13.17.

Luther was to lay central emphasis in his teaching on this Johannine insight, though the world thinks of Luther's theology as Pauline. It was Luther who differentiated sharply between general acceptance (*fides*) and total trust (*fiducia*). He could express himself more strongly still, not only as doing the truth, but more strongly as *to wager one's all on God*.[2]

John further deepened this truth in his special teaching on the Holy Spirit, recorded in the Supper discourses (Jn 4-17). The faithful disciple would have Christ with them permanently, as his Holy Spirit, to

---

[2] Pascal actually uses the same phrase, though I am not aware that he read Luther. They are both trustworthy guides and sound Christians.

lead them into the full truth (of living) when he had gone back to God, after the full completion of his ministry on earth.[3]

With v. 10, John resumes his exalted language. The Word was immanent in the world before the Incarnation; in fact, the world came into being through the Creative Logos and yet the world did not know him. (The text literally says "did not see the light," light here equivalent to the Word, the Light.)

Verse 11 says, he came, i.e. at a specific time, to a specific place, to his own chosen people in their own land, his own people, as promised and prophesied, to Palestine not Greece. Yet more is said. Israel did not receive him or accept him. Here is sounded that deep diapason of rejection at the very beginning. It runs throughout the entire Gospel, as it does through the prophets. It rings all down history, and rings in our ears today.

And yet, John states, there were some who did receive him, and whether Jew or Gentile, received the right to become "children of God" as believers. Already the gate of the Kingdom is open to all believers, all those who have faith in Christ, not simply those who believe his words, but those who believe *in* him. (John makes this same statement thirty-five times in his Gospel.) Beyond the whole process of nature, beyond any Jewish or other genealogy, beyond the action of the body, beyond any action of human will, they are brought to belief in Christ by the creative power of the Word (cf. Eph 2.8). It was the power, the divine energy, which empowered him to preach and teach the Word of God, empowered him to work miracles, the power which raised him from the dead, the power which carried him back to the right hand of God, the power which sustains and guides us in the Holy Spirit.

John now reaches the climax of his statement of Christ as the Word, "The Word became flesh." here the word "became" is too weak, but we do not have in English the right word. It is not only a misleading word, but it can be dangerous and deceiving. For example, it has bedevilled the later discussion of the Eucharistic theology, when theologians spoke of the bread and wine of the Communion service "becoming" the Body, "becoming" the Blood of Christ. What do

---

[3] I often ask myself how much the man or woman in the pew, or for that matter the man or woman in the pulpit, is aware of the might, the power, the majesty of these words. Now that the British Government has abolished lovely Christian Whitsuntide as a national holiday in favour of Labour Day and a bonus Bank Holiday, the half-believing populace has lost this valuable tradition. Even the name, Whitsunday, has gone. *Sic transit veritas.*

they mean by "become"? In the text under discussion, the word means "to come into existence," i.e. the eternal, indivisible Word came into existence in the flesh by creation. "Flesh" here means "human," not a "man," but the total, complete human being. Put simply, The Word came into existence as a human being.

The word "lived" in "lived among us," literally "tabernacled among us" is specially significant. To the Palestinian it meant but one thing, the dwelling of God right in the midst of the Hebrew people in the Tabernacle containing the ark of the covenant and the two tables of stone containing the Law. The Jews used the same word to mean the presence of God in the Temple. The Presence is now with them in Christ, in a unique complete and final form for humankind. He dwelt in our midst. God fulfilled his purpose in Creation by the Incarnation. He had fulfilled his promises - at great cost. More he could not have done. It is too good to be true: except that it is true.

John had seen all this with his own eyes, as had the disciples and apostles (the "we" of 1.14 and 21.34). This is the disciple who is bearing witness to these things *and who has written these things*: and we [disciples and apostles] *know* that his testimony is true, for they, too, were equally witnesses (Jn 21.24). This is testimony indeed.

John describes the Word as coming into existence among them full of grace and truth. Grace is the uniquely Christian word meaning the love and mercy of God seeking man's redemption, while truth to John is always associated with the Incarnation. This was the glory they all beheld.

The glory of God would mean to a Jew the majesty and effective power of God revealed in the history and worship of the Hebrew people, as experienced in the deliverance from slavery in Egypt, in the crossing of the Red Sea, in the ministry of Moses and the prophets, and in all their deliverances. To John it meant that this *heilsgeschichte* (the long story of their salvation by God) had now been fulfilled before their very eyes. This creates a new perspective, a deeper way of understanding. The Word that the disciples received from Jesus was no new thing; the strength of it was a fresh, original interpretation and fulfilment of a long-cherished hope. They saw everything with new eyes, for this interpretation "opened up the scriptures." It had its origins neither in ancient history, nor in the history of their own times, not even in the rhythm of creation. This Word was beyond space and time, beyond time and history; it belongs to eternity, and, therefore, to every epoch in time, to every race of humanity, to every man, every woman, every youth, every child. This Word never grows old and outworn. It never dates, neither does it burst forth into some new and novel idea. It is like the old wine, which everyone knows is far, far better than the new, any new. The Word of God is just what it is, the Word of God. No more can be said. In Jesus that Word became human; it came forth from God. More precisely, it came into existence as a human being, the human being for whom as a baby Mary tenderly cared, whom they knew and loved, and had given their all to follow, and who, in his ministry, had opened up the Kingdom of heaven to all believers. And all before their very eyes.

It is strengthening to recall the words of Heb 13.8, "Jesus Christ is the same yesterday, and today, and for ever," and to know that these mighty, empowering words of the prologue are as true to me (and you) as they were when the disciple wrote them and all the disciples and apostles endorsed them, and to reflect that "Christ is able for all time to save those who approach God through him" (Heb 7.25). It is a staggering but strengthening thought to know that Christ is praying for me (and for you, as you strive to understand), at this and every moment of the day and night. Christ is the permanent, ever present link to God, to eternal reality. He never changes.

The Incarnation is the unique, the only fact that explains Creation. It is the only reality that can explain God. A believer is given a glimpse of the mind and purpose of God, even a foretaste of heaven. It is that certainty, utterly objective, other than his own mind, utterly independent of the culture and fashions of the world, which gives the believer a certainty and conviction in the present life, in which he/she finds eternal life. Here again, indeed as always, John relates Creation and Incarnation.

It follows from this that we cannot understand and explain God in the terms of natural knowledge by means of reason. Reason properly and rightly explains the phenomena we experience on earth. These can be explained only in the natural language we develop to explain them. This knowledge is valid and verifiable. But such knowledge, perfectly true in itself, limits our enquiry to the area of physics, chemistry, mathematics, science generally. Not only is this knowledge of no avail when we seek to understand music, the arts, aesthetics generally, it cannot even explain the everyday human realities of our common life, e.g. love. More apt for our present argument, it certainly cannot explain or understand God. To do this we need objective and divine knowledge from the divine realm: a kind of "vertical" activity into our "horizontal" everyday activity. This Christ fulfils.[4] It is always difficult to convince the reasonable enquirer or critic *by reason* that reason in itself is inadequate to explain God, as it is equally inadequate to explain faith and belief, even all the aesthetic experiences of music, art and all the other lovely experiences this life affords.

John clearly states that God's Word ordered Creation with intent and purpose; that to fulfil this end he had called certain people to fulfil this purpose - Abraham, Moses; that he had existed before Abraham, and that Moses referred to him, again relating time and eternity to understand the course of history; that his chosen people proved faithless and unbelieving, bringing bitter mischief upon themselves. In his mercy he sent prophets to restore them by his Word, but Israel rejected them. All this is known, verifiable in their historical records.

John is saying that it is this same Word that came into existence as a human in Jesus the Christ, and further, within God's restraints, finalised and fulfilled the salvation history of the Jews for all mankind. To help us understand all this, John carefully preserves Christ's teaching and authority, namely, that while on earth as Jesus of Nazareth he still remained "in the bosom of the Father" (to quote Christ's own words), and that he "returned to the Father" after the Resurrection and Ascension, where he now lives, after graciously sending his Holy Spirit both to lead them to recall the full meaning of his ministry and to lead them to the full truth.

The language is clear, compelling, explicit, staggering though it be in its claims. It really takes the Trinitarian language of John to begin to comprehend the unfathomable depths of the inferences we are compelled to draw. The scholar's role is surely to study what Christ gave to John, his beloved disciple, and not explain it away in order to accommodate modern thinking; to bring moderns to learn the fact of Jesus, not to bring Christ to their level.

f. *Restoring Inter-Faith Understanding*

It is this theology, precisely on the meaning of the Incarnation, that occasioned the Great Refusal of the Jews, a tragedy from which Christendom – and indeed humanity – has yet to recover. Six hundred years later, Islam stumbled over the same stone, with far more deadly consequences, as the Western world experiences this Holy War at such terrible cost. Two thousand years later, our contemporaries baulk at this same theology. There was a time in the early days when Jews and

---

[4] The same thought of combination of wisdom and revelation is expressed in Eph 1.17. See p. 000.

Christians spoke as brothers. Equally, there have been times when Muslims and Christians lived together as brothers, even when at war (Saladin and Richard I). All this has gone. It is worth seeking to restore it, for the sake of truth, and above all, for the sake of mankind.

In addition to this specific task of inter-faith understanding and brotherhood, our task, which has always been the task of the Church, is to build up a specifically theological interpretation, with its own appropriate speech and language, to relate rationally and convincingly the divine realm to our everyday world, and to relate the implications and ramifications of incarnational theology to the world as discerned by rational mankind. This is what our great Church Fathers effected, the Cappadocian Fathers (Basil and the two Gregories), the Alexandrian Fathers (Clement, Origen, Athanasius, Cyril), the Latin Fathers (Irenaeus, Tertullian, Cyprian, and above all, the mighty Augustine); the Nicene and Constantinople fathers who in our creeds encapsulated this theology for all time, for all humanity, even to the extent of inventing new words with a larger meaning, lest the full truth be lost. They all sought, and with great success, to relate the interaction of the two worlds (realms, aions, spheres or what you will). Human language always lets us down in discussing the Incarnation. We may not have the language, but that does not matter. What does matter is, if we lose the truth, for that is what John is declaring, the Word's Word. The Word is in the bosom of the Father, active through the Holy Spirit in the hearts and minds of believing men and women. As also Paul taught, all the disciples and apostles, and the author of the Epistle to the Hebrews, too. That will prove the creative point of all new understanding.

It is this kind of creative thinking which the Incarnation opens up. It provides the clearest interaction of God with our (better his) created world and all within the framework of our own rationality and understanding. Expressed in these words, the Incarnation opens up, and will continue to open up for us in words of space/time, a true and creative understanding of our normal everyday life, life with God, in, through and even by means of all its hazards and uncertainties, its factions and tragedies, and finally death.

Further, there is a hidden bonus in this kind of thinking, for the new Physics is opening up great possibilities in its new thinking. Physicists and cosmologists now tread on theological ground as they seek their "Theory of Everything." With combined forces new thinking will be created in this area of incarnational thinking. (See Chapter 9.)

As long as people seem content to limit themselves to their own concepts and cerebrations, to what they can see and handle, weigh, measure, formulate - true and reliable though they be where applicable - they will dwell in their own self-chosen twilight. For what they are doing is limiting the world, the universe even, to their own insights, how they themselves see and interpret and understand everything. They restrict the world to their own mind. In other words, it is the individual's world, and not the Creator's: he is *as* God. It was on this very point that at the outset of human life, the "Tempter" corrupted natural Man (Adam) and it is at this point the natural, unredeemed person, remains deceived. (It is one way of explaining man's fundamental failing.) It is this intellectual and spiritual myopia that the Incarnation meets.

I knew the daughter of an American missionary to the Native Americans. She came to serve as a nurse during the Great War of 1914-18, and told me the following story. Her father, I am now speaking of the nineteenth century, met an old American Indian chief. The missionary was wearing spectacles. The chief asked him why he wore those things. The missionary replied, to help him see better. Intrigued, the Indian chief asked if the missionary would let him try them on. The chief was entranced with his new vision and refused to hand them back, begging to retain them. He now saw. He could never go back to his old half-sight. It is this that I want for the reader. In Christ he or she will see as never before. At the touch of Christ, the lame, the blind, the deaf, the lost and unwanted, even spiritual and intellectual leaders, were all made whole. The Incarnation offers the true wholeness of life to every man, woman, youth, child. You will find you cannot part with the spectacles of Christ.

It is from this prison house that the Incarnation was intended to deliver humankind, away from their natural self-centred, self-asserting interests (though these are natural and good, necessary for human evolution), to a new creation and a new freedom - nothing less. As soon as a person relates all his/her knowledge and all his/her activity to the theological field of the Incarnation, i.e. in and through Jesus Christ, he/she will begin to discover the open transcendental field of God as yielded by Christ. It is this transcendental reality alone that will give the true understanding of life, and at the same time, and this is important, preserve the natural man's natural understanding of everything. Our own historical transient existence is bound in a living, loving creative relationship to the eternal, loving objective reality of the living, eternal Christ, a reality that never changes, and which gives sense and meaning to the ever-changing meaninglessness of everyday life. Without this unchanging reliability and constancy in the eternal Christ, human culture prevails, and human culture can all too often express itself in war, hatred, crime and sin. Experience teaches us this hard, raw fact of human existence. In the Incarnation God offers us a new beginning. In fact, we could simply say that all that Christianity is about is a series of new beginnings.

In this sense God is actually giving us in Jesus Christ (i.e. in time and space), a divine point of reference. This enables us to see in Jesus Christ, and to find in that relationship, the true relationship between God and his Creation, and our authentic relationship to God. To quote Christ's own words, words the Jews so emphatically rejected (a measure of their truth), "he that has seen me has seen the Father" (Jn 14.9), "The Father and I are one and the same thing" (Jn 10.30) (own translations). It is this lovely relationship to the living Christ that provides for us human beings the *places of understanding*, where God meets man/woman in space and time, in the frailty and finitude of his/her brief, mortal existence. In this very finite and limited existence, he/she meets God, and knows him in his own being, and knows that all this is of his love, all is of his grace. We learn that this is the place where the heavenly and earthly meet, where humanity opens up to a transcendental God, where divinity penetrates humanity. All this is designed by God. We do handle not human ideas, but God's Word handles us.

The Incarnation provides us with the ultimate ontological explanation and experience of humanity's existence. By this I mean a Christian believer finds a new life, the old human life now enlarged with the presence of the divine in his/her mortal life. He/she exists in two dimensions, lives in two aions, not by virtue of his/her perception or education, but only by divine action. This can only be explained in terms of a wider epistemology, which yields a wholly new ontology. God in Christ, by the power of the Holy Spirit, has taken abode in the human heart, or, as Paul was to express it, If anyone is in Christ, he is a new creation. Without this relationship to God, humanity has no complete explanation of its place on earth, its meaning, its purpose, its end: with this, mankind is given meaning, purpose, end.

At the end of the Prologue (v. 18) John again breaks into prose, in describing the sober historical witnesses to his statements, namely Moses and the Law, John the Baptist, and "we all," i.e. John the Evangelist and the disciples and apostles, all of whom had received the grace, all of whom lived in and with the Holy Spirit. All these had lived in the two realms, the divine and the human: all addressed this earthly realm with words from the heavenly realm. And further, the phrase, "we all" includes all the believers who followed, i.e. "those who had not seen, yet believed" (Jn 20.29).

Last of all, and for the first time, Jesus is named, in association with Moses, standing for the Law and the prophets, and is described as the embodiment of grace and as the fulfilment of truth. No human has seen God, nor ever will. But Christ, in the bosom of the Father, he has explained and expounded him. Jesus gives us what he has seen and heard from God.

> I declare what I have seen in the Father's presence (8.38).
> I have told you the truth that I heard from God (8.40).
> Why do you not understand what I say? It is because you cannot accept my word (8.43).
> Because I tell the truth, you do not believe me (8.45).
> Whoever is from God hears the words of God. The reason you do not hear them is that you are not from God (8.47).

Here is the answer of the Fourth Evangelist to our problem of faith. God is invisible; he can neither be seen nor proved. The Word of God moves from its prophetic obscurity and invisibility to its objective seeable certainty in Christ. He is the adequate ground of faith. Christ declared once for all and explained God in person. We speak not of some vision, of some psychological, spiritual, mystical experience, but of a historical relationship between the disciples and the man Jesus. Unless the world - Jewish, Islamic and unbelievers alike - face this simple historic fact together, humbly and expectantly, they will never understand. Even the whole divine, loving purpose of God in his divine Creation could fizzle out at great pain and terrible cost, or at least be set back centuries at the hands of ignorant, misguided fanatics who think they can forward humanity's course with a few "divinely" guided rockets and a few judiciously placed missiles and a few bombs in chosen sites.

No. Let us sit down with the Jews, as we once did, and learn together what they think of these fresh views on old truths. Let us sit down with the Muslims, as once we used to do, and learn from them what they think of this fresh thinking on the meaning of the Incarnation. Let us sit down with the scientists, the unbelievers and all people of good will, and re-consider our positions. Truth has nothing to fear except the fear of being misunderstood. Would this not be a creative department of the United Nations? It could prove its worthiest, most creative and effective of all its departments.

g. *The First Commentators on St. John's Gospel*

In discussing the meanings of the word "Logos" at the beginning of this chapter, I stated that the later Jewish philosophers and Greek philosophers alike, whether they understood Logos as reason, or as meaning speech or word, were always concerned with Logos as revealing truth. But I also stated that they all found it difficult to find the right language to express the truth they were seeking in language we all use, for language is the only means we have of making or communicating meaningful thoughts and ideas. The problem was (and is): how to relate spirit and matter, the finite and the infinite, the one and the many, God and man. I there suggested that John in his Gospel links Creation with the Incarnation and this is decisive. He thereby relates God and man, Reason and Revelation, i.e. the Logos of the Creation with the Logos of the Incarnation, the Word which came into existence and dwelt among us, the Christ he saw, handled and heard, saw transfigured, saw resurrected and ascended. (To those who cynically say, And you believe a fisherman saw and wrote of these things, I would comment on what Heraclitus wrote, a mere slave, and what John Bunyan wrote, a mere tinker; or William Blake, a mere painter of tea pots in a cheap labour factory). They (Bunyan and Blake) just had one thing in common. They understood Christ. And John had lived with Jesus for three years; was Jesus' bosom companion; was chosen to experience the Transfiguration the Resurrection and Ascension; was one to whom, with the disciples, Jesus explained everything; and over a period of three years had been a full-time disciple.

It is important to bear in mind that John sees the Word as eternal, existent before Creation, the Creator of everything that exists, and as coming into existence in terms of flesh and blood in Jesus of Nazareth. John at once relates Creation and Incarnation.

I would argue that the Incarnation is the *only* means we have been given to explain and understand God and man, the Cosmos and our human existence, eternity and time, the infinite and the finite, indeed the meaning and purpose of our very existence. Creation started a process in time, even created Time, a process in which we are all involved, and as a process evolving in time, must have a purpose, a process in time, which must lead to a final fulfilment in Time. It is an ongoing process in which and of which we all partake. In other words, the purpose of history can only be fulfilled in the Last Day of Time, the end of time. And, as St. Paul conceived it in Ephesians, Christ called all believers to complete and fulfil his ministry.

It is this eternal cosmic nature of Christ that I seek to express, with a view to recapturing it for the Church, the Kingdom of all believers. This is the dimension in which Paul, John and Hebrews expressed their thinking. I seek to remind us of the eternal, cosmic Christ, the divine constant, immanent and imminent in the universe, his significance for, and relatedness to, all mankind, the meaning for ourselves.

To this end I here introduce to the reader my studies of the great commentaries on St. John's Gospel by the early Fathers, who, I found, show an affinity to St. John's mind and writing not always found by liberal modern commentators (their great learning notwithstanding), with their modern concern for the *ignis fatuus,* of "literal" truth.

The Didactic Structure of St John's Gospel
It is known to us all that John (the author of St. John's Gospel) records seven "signs" of Jesus, and further seven "I am" sayings. They are:

The Seven Signs
The turning of water into wine (2.1-11)
The healing of the nobleman's son (4.46-54)
The healing of the impotent man (5.2-9)
The feeding of the five thousand (6.4-13)
The walking on the water (6.16-21)
The healing of the man born blind (9.1-7)
The raising of Lazarus (11.1-54)

The Seven "I am" … sayings
I am the Bread of Life (6.35)
I am the Light of the World (8.12)
I am the Door of the Sheepfold (10.7)
I am the Good Shepherd (10.11)
I am the Resurrection and the Life (11.25)
I am the Way, the Truth and the Life (14.6)
I am the True Vine (15.1)

It is difficult to see any distinctive progression of thought running through the series, and commentators ancient and modern interpret them in their own individual way, as perhaps John meant us to see and understand and grow in our own understanding. When all is said, St. John closes his Gospel with these words:

> But there are also many other things which Jesus did; if every one of them were written down, I suppose that the world itself could not contain the books that would be written (Jn 21.25).

I take this to mean that the holy number of seven signs and seven sayings are wholly adequate to reach the truth on this earthly pilgrimage.

Let us now take a brief look at how the earliest commentators expounded these incidents (signs) and sayings for they are much closer to the mind of John than we moderns are.

The Earliest Commentators on St. John's Gospel

There are references to St. John's Gospel in the Apostolic Fathers[5] and in the Apologists[6] but I draw attention to those who wrote a commentary on the Gospel as a guide towards understanding how the first commentators understood and interpreted St. John's account of Christ. It is in no way a summary of these commentaries, but rather a light on how they read John in those early days. They are in order:

Heracleon (c. 145 – c. 180) as extant

Origen (c. 195 – c. 254) as extant

Cyril of Alexandria (d. 444)

Chrysostom (c. 347 - 407)

Augustine (354 - 430).[7]

i. The Commentary of Heracleon

This commentary on St. John's Gospel, which we now have only in the fragments quoted by Origen (fairly quoted by Origen *verbatim*), has the fundamental weakness (mentioned by Origen) that he interprets the Gospel from Gnostic presuppositions which pre-judge his conclusions. This is a perfectly valid criticism, for Heracleon sees a symbolic significance in all personages, places, events, and statements. Nevertheless, he did see the profundity of St. John's Gospel, and that John was doing more than presenting a narration. It remains true that he understands that John presents Man in different stages of intellectual and spiritual conviction confronted by Christ, the Word of God. The incident, whether it is the Samaritan woman or the nobleman, for instance, is always and invariably interpreted as the soul of humankind

---

[5] Those Fathers of the period immediately succeeding the Apostles, namely, and mainly, Clement of Rome, Ignatius, Hermas, Polycarp, Barnabas, Diognetus, and the *Didache*. Some of these writings nearly got into our New Testament Canon.

[6] The name given to those writers (between AD 120 and 220) who first addressed the educated of this period, submitting their own explanation (Apologia) of Christianity. They were Aristides, Justin Martyr, Tatian, Athenagoras, Theophilus, Minutius Felix, and Tertullian.

[7] The commentary of Theodore of Mopsuestia (c. 350–428) proved inaccessible.

in a certain condition confronted by God himself in Christ, and is never related as a mere particular historical incident of a person meeting Jesus. His fatal weakness is that he interprets everything from Gnostic presuppositions, as did the rejected apocryphal gospels.

It is significant for Heracleon that not only the historical facts which constitute the Gospel, but also the tiniest details of the facts are made to carry a further meaning to the incident – even the shoes worn carry an evangelical significance. If it be remembered that Heracleon was a Gnostic, and that Gnostics came to the Gospel records for support of a gospel of salvation which they already believed on grounds other than the Christian revelation, and with little regard for the plain historical facts, a still further significance is given to his detailed handling of the text in such an evangelical manner. Quite certainly, Heracleon believed that the Fourth Evangelist furnished his detail with the intent of conveying a further meaning to the incident. He may be wrong about the meaning drawn, as he sometimes was, but right in his understanding that John intended an evangelical meaning to be inferred from the narratives he selects (selected from the many other incidents "that if every one of them were to be written down, I suppose that the world itself could not contain the books that would be written" (Jn 21.25). What is certain is that this early commentator saw that John selected his incidents with intent, and that our task is to find out that intent.

ii. *The Commentary of Origen* (as extant)

Not unlike Heracleon, Origen expounds the episodes of the Fourth Gospel as human beings in their varying states of spiritual need or intellectual doubt, and in that state of mind confronted by Christ. Origen has, of course, other principles guiding his exegesis, including the rebuttal of Gnosticism on scriptural grounds; the justifying of Christianity as against Judaism, also on scriptural grounds; a deep concern to explain any scriptural passage in its plain, grammatical sense; and a pastoral tendency to draw a moral for living. In other words he was addressing his own particular environment and its needs.

Let us consider some examples of how he handled certain incidents and personages of the Gospel. The first sign, the changing of the water into wine, is interpreted as: in the fullness of time, and the Law and the prophets having performed their office, Jesus, the true and expected Messiah has come bringing the good wine of the Kingdom of heaven. (The good wine was the traditional sign of the coming of the Messiah, and would be considered in no other way by a Jew.) Jesus' first sign was to superannuate Judaism.

The Cleansing of the Temple, following immediately after, indicates that the Temple has now served its purpose and is no longer needed. Christ swept it away and offers the Gospel. The Gospel, and not the Law, is alone adequate to human salvation.

Origen interprets the meeting of the Samaritan by the well of Jacob as the soul of man unable to find satisfaction in Judaism, ever seeking to assuage its natural spiritual thirst, and ever continuing to find the well of Judaism unable to meet its need. Christ comes and certainly and finally settles the thirst of the soul.

In the incident of the nobleman's son, Origen simply says the nobleman was Abraham, and his son (Israel) about to die, and who without Christ will die, and that Christ restores him to life. Christ is Israel's salvation. Israel is now transformed into the true Israel, i.e. the Christian believers. Note carefully Origen's continual concern to show that Christ was the fulfilment of Judaism.

In the Raising of Lazarus, every character in the episode is considered as a spiritual type - Mary is the contemplative one, Martha the active worker. But the central figure, Lazarus, is interpreted deliberately and in detail as the type of "Man-soul." He is the soul lapsed from faith and alienated from Christ (who is absent from the scene, far away). Consequently, he falls sick, and dies. Christ comes and raises his soul to life again. However, even when restored, Lazarus has his grave clothes clinging to him, meaning that he is still liable to sin and die again.

But it is not only to the incidents that Origen gives a symbolic interpretation, but to personages, dates, times, numbers; he sees a further meaning in everything. Andrew is the missionary, John the type of pure discipleship, Peter the type of faith and action.

The feasts are the earthly types of what heaven has yet to offer us. Origen refers to three Passovers:

> that which gave to the ancient children of Israel deliverance from their earthly enemy at the hand of Moses;
> that which gave to the New Israel (the Church) deliverance from their spiritual enemy, by the redemption effected by Christ;
> that which will be celebrated with myriads of angels.

The incidental detail is rich beyond assessment, as might have been expected, but only a few of the suggestive details are recapitulated here.

Christ's shoes were allegorized and signified his Incarnation. The harvest was the harvest of truth. Capernaum was a journey down, but Jerusalem a journey up. Moses and the prophets were the sowers, the Apostles the reapers. Not a single detail escaped comment by Origen, even down to the use of particular prepositions, and the presence or absence of the article. "It was night" (Jn 13.30) is the darkness into which Judas plunged his soul.

In this connection too, his typological exposition of the Old Testament must be noticed. Abraham's history is the allegory of man's salvation. The crossing of the Red Sea and the entry into the promised Land all prefigure and typify man's salvation and his entry into the Kingdom of heaven.

It is true that all scripture lends itself to spiritual interpretation, and all its incidents and details can be made to bear a message. Indeed this has been the basis of both hymnody and homiletics. Further, the same technique enjoyed universal application by the Fathers (with the natural and obvious exception of the teaching of Jesus which was expounded in its real and intended meaning). But in the particular case of the Fourth Gospel, it is no simple spiritualizing as such, as for instance in the case of the exposition of the Good Samaritan in Augustine. It is not a merely original and valuable eliciting of truth: it is the stark confrontation of man with truth itself. To Origen, John has a single and simple principle unifying his selection of incidents and events. Christ had come in the fullness of time, prepared from the Creation of the world as God's Last Word to man. Man, in all his conditions, is confronted by God made Flesh. Man's answer is final and determinative for now and all time. God has spoken in flesh and blood. What is man's reply? What is his reader's reply? John himself has seen the eternal significance of the Incarnation, and nothing matters more than that man should have this presented to him, and in a way in which he could see and understand. Every incident, and for the commentators if not for John himself every detail as well, subserves his intent, so that man in his varying spiritual conditions may perhaps see, believe, and have life eternal. So Origen understood John, and quite possibly John meant himself to be understood.

Origen's exegesis is regrettably incomplete, but there is sufficient evidence to indicate that his exegesis of the Fourth Gospel was a typological and spiritual exposition of the soul of man in its varying conditions or experiences, sometimes sick, sometimes lost, sometimes even dead, but always with a possibility of restoration in Christ. In Origen's exegesis, the soul of man has been elevated but never saved by Judaism. But even so, this is a true interpretation of the emphasis that the Fourth Evangelist had himself made.

iii. *The Commentary of Cyril of Alexandria*

To Cyril the Fourth Gospel was strictly historical in every detail, but to him it was history with a meaning. He does not indulge in the flights of fancy of other Alexandrines, for he has a sober and strict historical sense, but this makes his spiritualizing of the events even more effective. There is the strictest regard for the history, but all of the events carry a deep spiritual significance, which he gives or suggests in the most quiet terms. The present author maintains both that such was the intention of the Evangelist, and also that these early commentators have so interpreted St. John's Gospel.

The Marriage at Cana teaches the coming of Christ in the fulfilment of time. It is a parable of the Incarnation and an allegory of man's redemption. The water of the Law is changed into the new spiritual power of the Gospel, intoxicating man and giving him a new spirit.

The Cleansing of the Temple is interpreted as the rejection of the Jews and further, the turning of God's Messiah, unwanted by God's people, to the Gentiles.

Nicodemus is the rejection of Judaism at its loftiest. In him Cyril teaches the typological history of the Jews, and the defeat of sin only in Christ, who alone brings salvation. Judaism is condemned not by Christ, but by itself.

The Samaritan Woman is the finding of the Messiah by the Gentile mind. It is a critical point. Christ cannot win those to whom he was sent and he turns to the outside world.

The nobleman whose son was sick meant for Cyril the mind that was really ignorant but yet had faith enough to seek out Christ.

The Impotent Man is man in the grip of Judaism, impotent, and waiting for "a man" to put him into the pool and therefore save him. "The man" who came was Christ. Judaism, meant to prepare the way for Christ, yet held the Jews spiritually impotent and needing truly Jesus to deliver them.

The feeding of the multitude is a pure allegory of the Eucharist set against the Old Testament background of the history of the Israelites. Christ was alone the True Bread, and the Jews could not understand the significance of their own history and God's dealings with them, neither in Moses' day, nor in Christ's. The theme, the failure of the Jews to understand, runs throughout Cyril's commentary.

The man born blind is treated as an allegory of the soul's ignorance of God, and the theme of blindness is made to apply to the Jewish attitude to Christ whom God had sent.

Christ alone is the Good Shepherd, for only he can lead and save the sheep.

Lazarus is the soul of man dead because Christ is absent. The soul is restored to life when the Master is present.

The rest of the narrative consists of the supper discourses and the passion narrative, and the incidents as such end with Lazarus. But a few words could be added on Cyril's attitude to the disciples.

They were, of course, considered purely as historical personages, but he spiritualizes their characteristics, e.g. in the calling of the disciples and also the striking off of Malchus's ear by Peter "given as a pattern expressly for our learning" (Jn 18.10).

Cyril was writing to combat error and maintain orthodox Christianity, and therefore made a limited and qualified use of allegory and spiritualization. Orthodoxy to Cyril meant in the main:

> a true and firm hold of the meaning of scripture; and
> a full allegiance to the Christian Society and the receiving of Christ in the Eucharist.

The Fourth Gospel was the perfect weapon in this battle. It was both the key to the scriptures and also the sanction for sacramental union with Christ in the fellowship of the Church. For that reason, Cyril's commentary is his greatest work.

His exegesis of the Fourth Gospel lends much support to the contention of the present study though not to the same extent as Origen. But Origen did not have the same dogmatic battle to win; he had a freer pen, and his work is in a sense "less responsible."

Cyril makes the incidents and episodes bear some spiritual interpretation, as the above examination shows. It would seem fair to maintain that Cyril believed the Fourth Gospel to have an intended spiritual interpretation, and whatever value we assess to his discernment of it, it is important to realize that Cyril did understand the Fourth Evangelist to have this further intent, and also that he never lost sight of this, even though he was engaged on what he thought was primarily an elucidation of Christian doctrine.

iv. *The Commentary of Chrysostom*
To Chrysostom the plain, historical, grammatical and literal sense of Scripture was the primary and almost exclusive one. Even in places such as "It was night" (Jn 13.30), wherein every commentator has seen a spiritual significance, Chrysostom stubbornly interprets this in its primary sense of fact - it was night, and that was the fact.

Chrysostom lends little support to the seeking of interpretative principles in the early commentators. Indeed, the entire school of Antioch stands utterly apart. The school made a great contribution to biblical studies, and the reading of their comments and criticisms is singularly modern and refreshing. It produced a valuable balance to the rather unpredictable exegesis of the allegorical schools.

But it had great failings. It was insensitive to all the colour of Christ's teaching, his poetry and paradox. The Bible after all is not mere history, but the interpretation of history, and that in the special sense of God's action in history. The historical and philological techniques are essential to any true exegesis, but unaided they yield impoverished and barren conclusions. Indeed many modern commentaries stop short here, and Hoskyns produced a much-needed stimulus to theological exposition in his commentary. Without insight into the spirit and meaning of a passage, grammar and logic defeat their purpose.

A close reading of Chrysostom, however, shows that he was in no sense bound to the literal technique, and as indicated in the text, often gave an allegorical or spiritual interpretation. Before discussing the Johannine incidents, it is worth mentioning a few instances of his spiritual interpretation. For example, he contrasts the disciples and speaks of them as types, e.g. in the cases of Nathaniel and Nicodemus and in the discussion of the Samaritan Woman and her comparison with the Jews. Light and darkness are considered as truth on the one hand, and sin and error on the other. He interprets history as a type of Christian salvation, e.g. in the deliverances from Egypt, the story of the Passover and other details of Jewish history. The significance of the riding on the ass is not merely to show humility but the subjection of the Gentiles to him. The footwashing means the washing of consciences. In Jn 16.16 childbirth is given a mystical interpretation. All these instances show that even Chrysostom used the allegorical or spiritual interpretation. (They are in no sense exhaustive, but are simple instances which occur to the memory.) With Chrysostom, however, one has the feeling that he never goes further in his spiritual interpretation than Scripture had already gone before him, in, for example, Paul and his interpretation of the Old Testament, and also in John and in Hebrews. Though the spiritual interpretation is not marked or even obvious, it is yet there, but limited and guarded.

To examine the Johannine incidents:

The Water and the Wine

As Jesus worked then, changing water into wine, so the new life, created in us by the living Christ, is still changing our weak and unstable wills that they may be no longer wishy-washy (*diarrhein* - our word diarrhoea!) but have body (*epistummenon*), and in the change bring gladness to ourselves and others. The watery people are those of this world.

The Cleansing of the Temple

This incident is expounded as an historical event without any spiritualizing.

Nicodemus

Chrysostom speaks of Nicodemus entangled in Jewish infirmity, coming to Jesus by night, and failing to learn because of asking the wrong question. Only a cleansed life, illuminated by the light of knowledge, can understand Christ.

He develops the incident as an exposition of baptism, and discusses the Old Testament types in much detail. Here he declares that Nicodemus's real sin is unbelief, and moves on to consider unbelief and its effects on the human soul. He does not say that Nicodemus is a type of the human soul, but certainly considers him as such.

The Samaritan Woman

He compares her very favourably with Nicodemus and also with Jewry. Neither have the desire to learn, which she shows. He even chides his listeners with the same condemnation. Chrysostom expounds the passage to indicate that what the woman was seeking was spiritual things, and it was precisely to those that Christ was leading her. Water as such is not discussed at all. Further, the field and the harvest indicate souls ready for salvation. He also makes the point of the real connection between the Old Testament and the New Testament, for the prophets had done much of the sowing. The whole incident is expounded as the soul's seeking for truth, which is its salvation, and which is given by Christ. This exposition is very similar to that of most of the Fathers.

The Nobleman's Son

Chrysostom emphasizes the cure of the nobleman rather than his son and this is significant. The value of the sign lay not in the cure of the physical disease of the son, but in the cure of the spiritual disease of the father - the disease of half-belief, or even unbelief. Christ showed here that his real purpose was to heal the sick in mind by his teaching, and that his real care was for souls rather than bodies.

The Impotent Man

At the outset, Chrysostom describes the incident as a mystery, signifying baptism in type and figure. Just as the water needed an angel, so also the water of baptism needs the Spirit. The miracle was to show that Christ's desire was to cure souls. The 38 years is spiritualized.

The disease had been produced by the man's sins. It was the man's sin that was being removed by the work of Christ, and his cure was complete, for he walked by himself.

The incident is treated as the salvation of a man in sin by the coming of Christ to cure him.

The Feeding of the Five Thousand

The important part of Christ's work lies in the discourses and sermons; the signs are given for people of lower spiritual discernment, i.e. they are meant to teach and signify something other than they were.

Chrysostom here actually spiritualizes Christ's journey to Jerusalem from Galilee as a sign that he was annulling the Law.

He draws parallels with Moses and Elisha to emphasize the didactic significance of the sign. In other words, the event is spiritualized - as of course the Evangelist meant it to be.

The Jews in their obtuseness do not see the spiritual teaching, but keep their mind on manna. But manna was a type and not the truth, and the truth was Christ.

This truth Chrysostom interprets in two ways: first, faith in him and his teaching; and second, receiving of him in the Eucharist. Both are equally taught, although more time is given to the latter. He refers here to the blood in the Old Testament frightening away death at the Passover as the figure of Christ's blood destroying death for the believer. This teaching, of the believer receiving Christ's Body and Blood, he describes as fact and not enigma. God had fed the Jews for forty years without harvest or corn. Now, under the New Covenant, he will feed his children and give them not merely long days but eternal life. Such words are of no profit to the carnally minded.

The Man born blind

Many of the details in the incident are made to carry a spiritual significance, e.g. the clay and the spittle, and the pool Siloam, and are examined in their place.

Chrysostom says that the real work of God is bringing faith to the human individual, and this is the significance of Christ giving sight. It is in this context that the incident is interpreted.

Again, it is revealing to find Chrysostom giving the historical incident a spiritual meaning.

Lazarus

The incident is interpreted historically. Spiritual truth is drawn from the incident, but the event itself is not "spiritualized," perhaps because of the importance of safeguarding the historicity of the event.

v. *The Commentary of St. Augustine*

Finally, we turn to the last and the greatest of our earliest commentators, St. Augustine. Everyone knows of his conversion in the garden, when, on hearing a little girl begging her mother to pick up the book and read to her, he picked up the Book at his side (the Bible) to read, "Put on the Lord Jesus Christ" (Rom 13.14), and of the last conversation he had with his mother, Monica, at Ostia where she died saying her one wish had been granted in that Augustine was now a Christian. Augustine was now thirty-three years old.

Augustine is certainly the greatest Latin Father, perhaps the greatest theologian of all time. His influence dominated mediaeval Christianity in the West, where he became one of the four "Doctors" of the Church. He influenced Protestantism through Luther, and for both Catholicism and Protestantism he remains a major resource. It could even be argued that every revival of Christianity from then to the present day has been Augustinian. Let us now turn to his commentary on St. John's Gospel.

His opening words commenting on Jn 1.1-5 declare at once his theological approach. He writes, "as lofty mountains are the first to reflect the light of the sun, so John the Evangelist was one of the elevated souls first to receive and then to reflect the Light of Truth." He emphasizes that such souls only reflect the light and are not the Light themselves.

He describes Christ as *God's* Idea, his Word, the inner word made known in act. A carpenter has an idea of a chest and makes one; the chest decays. But the idea remains. In such a way *"God's Idea"* may be understood. (This is highly Platonic.)

He goes on to say that the Word of God was not made, for by it were all things created being made. The life of all created things is in the Word, as the living idea is in the mind of the artist. The Word is the light of rational man, seen only by the pure in heart. The natural person cannot see this life in Christ. Just as a man blinded by dust cannot see, so man, because he/she is blinded by sin, cannot see spiritually. Here one sees the entire Gospel expressed in a few words, furthering the idea that there are those who see and understand and those who can neither see nor understand. The point he makes at the outset, that the Word is "God's Idea," is specially important for the argument of this book. (See Chapters 1 and 2.)

Augustine's Exegesis of the Episodes of the Fourth Gospel

John the Baptist

John the Baptist is considered as the summing up of all prophecy and in *Hom*. IV. 7, Augustine actually sums up John the Baptist's words, "I am prophecy itself."

The Calling of the Disciples

Augustine's handling of the call of the disciples is revealing (*Hom*. VII). He says that the two disciples have already been called by the lakeside. The incident therefore means more than this calling of the disciples, which has already taken place. The two disciples follow at the tenth hour, and that means they have reached the end of the commandments and are following therefore a new master, who will give a new law, and with whom they seek to abide.

Simon's name was changed to Petra, and in his name the Church was foreshadowed; and no one is safe except for those he that build on this rock (Mt 7.24-27). Augustine interprets the changing of Simon's name didactically.

Nathaniel was not chosen as a disciple because he was learned in the Law, but for other reasons. (Modern scholars identify Nathaniel with Bartholomew but not so the ancients, Augustine, Chrysostom, Gregory of Nyssa etc.) Referring to Ps 65.4, Augustine explains that the Lord did choose orators, but only after he had chosen fishermen; rich men, only after he had chosen poor men; emperors, only after workers, lest all of these should think they were chosen for the merits of scholarship or wealth and the like. Nathaniel was under the shadow of death under the fig tree, for the fig leaf indicates sin (Gen 3.7). The incident is interpreted as meaning the seeking out of the true Israel. The seeking out of Nathaniel was Christ redeeming mankind, which was lying under the condemnation of sin. Nathaniel he interprets as the calling of the Church. The Church, the True Israel, are the people living by faith.

Even the name of Malchus, the servant of the High Priest, is mentioned by the Evangelist with a purpose, for Malchus means "he who reigns." In other words, when the old hearing is cut away, and a new hearing restored by Christ, then that person will reign with him (*Hom.* CXII).

In *Hom.* CXXIV John actually says, in speaking of Peter and John, that Peter was the type of action, and John the type of contemplation.

The Changing of the Water into Wine

In this sign there is at once something mysterious and sacramental. Augustine deplores the fact that people look at the miracle rather than its meaning, and this in itself is a good point for this book. To consider the sign as an historical event without interpretation, Augustine describes as turning one's back to God.

The central theme of the sign is Christ's coming in the flesh. The conversion of the water to wine is the conversion of the flat, insipid drink of the scriptures converted into the new intoxicating Spirit-filled drink of Christ.

He describes in detail the whole history of man from Adam, showing God's redemptive power at work from that time. The opening of Adam's side when Eve, the mother of all living, was born, prefigured the opening of Christ's side when the life-giving Sacraments issued forth. As Noah once saved the world by wood (the Ark), so Christ now saves the world by wood (the Cross). Every detail carries an evangelical significance.

The present writer suggests that this was precisely the intent of the Fourth Evangelist, and the tedious and repetitive discussions on the historicity of the event on the part of some modern interpreters bring a fog where once was clarity of vision. R.G. Collingwood in his autobiography maintained that true knowledge is a process of question and answer, and the important issue is to ask the right question. It is obvious that the ancient commentators were more sensitive to the real issues of interpretation that have been many of our moderns, and had the art of asking the right questions, as far as the intent of the Fourth Evangelist goes.

Whatever value is set on Augustine's conclusions is a matter of personal judgment. The real issue for the present discussion is whether his technique is right and also whether the Fourth Evangelist intended his work so to be understood. The present writer would answer in the affirmative to both questions.

The Cleansing of the Temple

The natural details of the incident are moralized upon in the obvious way of cleansing of the Church of all self-seekers. The deeper significance of the event is made to bear a soteriological redemptive significance. The Temple is Adam, mankind unredeemed and ultimately destroyed, but by Christ redeemed and restored to full communion with God.

Nicodemus

In the coming of Nicodemus the Pharisee to Jesus by night, Augustine sees the coming of Israel from its darkness to the light of Christ. Augustine gives an account of the journey of Israel from bondage in Egypt to the promised Land. The enemy slain in the Red Sea is the destruction of sin in baptism consecrated by Christ's blood. Their receiving manna in the wilderness is the Christian's receiving of the True Bread of Life. He says that this is what Christ meant, but being in the flesh Nicodemus cannot hear the Spirit. Augustine goes on to show the two streams in the people of Israel, the free and the bond, though both of the same seed. He gives as examples Sarah and Hagar, and Jacob and Esau.

He continues the history of Israel. As they lay in the desert dying from the bite of serpents and were saved from *temporal death* by the elevation of the serpent, so the true Israel dying from sin is brought to *eternal life* by the cross which was the true reality of which Moses' serpent was the figure (see Num 21.4-9).

Nicodemus is handled by Augustine as the type of Israel. Nicodemus's difficulties are our own difficulties, too. The Evangelist is at pains to show that Nicodemus failed to understand and emphasizes why, so that the reader may not remain in the same darkness. The Evangelist is not primarily concerned with Nicodemus, who merely passes out of the episode, but is deeply concerned that the reader may understand. This was John's technique, and Augustine saw this crystal clear.

The Samaritan Woman

To Augustine, the Samaritan Woman indicates the coming of the Church to its Saviour. Devoid of reason (her lawful husband), and in the grip of lusts which never satisfy her, she cannot come to Christ until reason has sway, and lust is removed. When she heard and learned Christ, she flung away lust, and preached Christ. (Augustine's emphasis on reason is most refreshing.)

The episode is treated as the pilgrimage of the soul to Christ, and the effect of Christ, when he is understood. (The exegesis is almost autobiographical.)

The thought of the exegesis centres round the Incarnation and the Redemption, when considering the divine aspect; and when considering the human aspect, it centres on the experience of the human soul in its ignorance and sin confronted by its real Lord. Indeed, the incident is made to tell this story, and though we may not care to go as far as Augustine (in interpreting, for example, the five husbands or the two days he stayed with the Samaritans), it seems to me that it was this story that the Fourth Evangelist was actually telling, and not the mere incident of the woman at the well, and that Augustine rightly so discerned it.

The Healing of the Nobleman's Son

Augustine seems to draw from this incident only that the Samaritans believed in Christ without a miracle, but not his own people; and he likens the Samaritans to the Gentiles who accept Christ not having seen a miracle, and the Galileans, his own people, to the Jews.

Origen and Heracleon made a great deal out of this incident, interpreting it as the salvation of Israel. Augustine seems only to draw a moral and not develop any real soteriological significance.

The Impotent Man

The impotent man is Jewry, shut in by the Law and waiting for the spiritual power of Jesus. The man he waited for was Jesus Christ, who released him from his impotency and set him on his journey.

The Feeding of the Five Thousand

This incident is made to tell the redemption of Israel. Israel is in great hunger, and its own scriptures (the loaves) which were meant to feed, are but a burden to them (i.e. carried). Though the grain of the bread is hard to get at (which is true of barley), Christ performed the work, and in so doing opened up the whole meaning of God's redemptive work in history. The people under the Law are carnally minded (sitting on the ground) receive the bread, and their hunger is alleviated. Christ makes plain the meaning of the story of Israel, and then a great and new Israel is born and nourished at his hand.

The Walking on the Water

This is interpreted as the coming of Christ to a Church tossed and troubled, and in darkness. He also makes the incident convey the idea that finally, when the Law is fulfilled, Christ comes to those who have fully kept the Law.

The Man Born Blind

The man born blind is mankind in general, born blind by original sin. The coming of Christ cleanses man and restores his/her sight. After being washed and cleansed by Baptism in Christ (the Sent One, i.e. Siloam), the man is now in a condition to show belief in Christ. This is the story of everyone's pilgrimage: everyone is born a sinner and therefore is blind. Only Christ coming to earth (the significance of the clay and spittle), can restore to man his sight. To this passage is sub-joined the teaching of the sheep, the brigands and the shepherd. The fold is the Church and one can enter only through Christ.

The Raising of Lazarus

Augustine interprets the restoring of the dead as the resurrection of the soul, dead through sin. He handles the varying states of death and its causes, showing how God never denies mercy. It is the resurrection of our soul that is being discussed.

Lazarus is the habitual sinner far gone in his sin; so far gone, that he actually is rotten and stinks, and has thereby alienated himself from God, who therefore cannot find him. From this sleep, God in his mercy raises him. Augustine beseeches his hearers over and over again to realize that he is not speaking to them about the mere Raising of Lazarus, but is begging them to take heed and understand that the incident speaks of their own soul dying in sin. Their conscience must be stirred and troubled, and in that groaning their faith would be res-urrected and they would live again. He actually equates faith with life.

This incident is the climax of the Fourth Gospel, though of course it is not so in the Synoptics. It is bound to be the Johannine climax, for hitherto John has recorded the soul of man in its various conditions confronted by God's word: the good, orthodox, yet closed mind of Nicodemus; the superstitious, ignorant, yet open mind of the Samari-tan woman; the indifferent, worldly mind of the soldier, who is yet willing to believe; the secluded mind of the impotent man unwilling to believe; the ever-present rebellious Jews resisting God's Word; na-ture yielding to it: the mind of the materialist, satisfied with bread and wanting therefore a king of this sort; the idealist, though not under-standing fully, yet perseveres as many turn back; the multitude, untouched and unconvicted; the sinner, convicted; man in his blindness; man without God dying and therefore reaching what is the last experience of our mortal life.

Lazarus is the only turning point such a Gospel could have. Indeed, after Lazarus, the only sequel was for the High Priest to command Christ's death.

The rest of the Gospel is Christ's being, his teaching and his rejection, and the story of those eight days when man slowly realized that truth could not be slain and that nothing mattered so much as our perception of this.

In the telling of the significance of the details of the Passion narrative, Augustine rises to great heights. The obvious signs, such as the seamless robe and the piercing of Christ's side giving birth to the Sacraments, are discussed, but even details such as the vinegar (the Jews who are the wine of the patriarchs and the prophets gone bad), come under his eagle eye. In this connection almost all commentators have seen that the detail in the Passion narrative was intended to bear a significance beyond that of simple descriptive fact, and indeed of a peculiar and particular evangelical and soteriological significance. What has been generally recognized as a true technique in expounding the meaning of the Passion narrative, has not been generally recognized as a true technique in expounding the meaning of the rest of the Gospel.

To discuss all these points in any detail would be to re-present the evidence adduced earlier in this section. Suffice it to say, that all of these incidents, episodes and details are made to bear an evangelical significance. John may never have intended all the specific meanings adduced by ancient commentators, and quite possibly Origen was right in saying that the only one ever to understand fully the Fourth Gospel will be another son of Mary (as John), and one who (as John) has lain in Christ's bosom, but it seems difficult and profitless to deny that John had this further intent, and the task of the commentator is to plumb John's depth. The ancient commentators give overwhelming evidence that they believed John to have written with this further intent.

These extracts show, not only how our early scholars understood St. John's Gospel, invaluable as that is, but also, I am suggesting, that standing nearer to John himself, these early commentators remind us moderns of the true lines on which we may understand John. They certainly lend a deeper understanding to St John's interpretation of the Incarnation in his Gospel.

The following texts were examined in this study of the earlier commentators on St. John's Gospel:

A.E. Brooke, *Heracleon: Texts and Studies*, vol. I, no. 4 (Cambridge, 1891); A.E. Brooke, *Origen: In Evangelium Joannis* (Cambridge, 1896); E.B. Pusey, *Cyril. In D. Joannis Evangelium* (Oxford, 1872); *Chrysostom. Homiliae in Joannis Evangelium*, Montfaucon (Paris, 1836); J.P. Migne, *Augustine. In Joannis Evangelium*, Texts and Studies, Patrologia, 414-416/417. (The two last-named texts may be found in translation in the Library of the Fathers.)

The reader will readily see for him/herself that these early commentators on St. John's Gospel, each in their own way, and each in their own day, interpreted the meaning and message of the Incarnate Lord as he confronted humankind in all its brokenness - the learned and the lost; the sick and the poor; the helpless and the hopeless; the ruler and the servant; even the dead. He meets that as God's representative, no less, God's messenger to all men and women. These early commentators often seem closer to the mind and purpose of Christ than some modern commentators, and perhaps closer to the mind of Christ, too. They all certainly found God's meaning and purpose in the Incarnation. None sought to explain it away. They sought to understand the unique event of the Incarnation, and to explain it to their contemporaries. They knew that in Jesus Christ God had visited and redeemed his people. And that is what the Incarnation means. Just that.

4

The Incarnation according to St. Paul

a. St. Paul's Apprenticeship

To turn from the mind of John to the mind of Paul is to go through a moving, creative, spiritual and intellectual experience.

John, a deeply religious young man, first appears as a disciple of John the Baptist, and is persuaded by John's preaching that Jesus is the Messiah. After three years with Jesus he grows into the status of being Christ's most trusted disciple, almost his confidante. He sits close to him at that Last Supper to hear all those final discourses. He stands by Jesus at the Cross, where Jesus commits his mother to his care after his death. He is the first disciple at the empty tomb, "he saw and believed," a witness of the Ascension and final commission. The disciple "whom Jesus loved" tells the story of that divine love in his Gospel, as he experienced it, and what it means for all mankind.

How different the apprenticeship of Paul! his convictions as a Jewish scholar brought him into violent rebellious opposition. While engaged on what were murderous activities (e.g. the stoning of Stephen), he was confronted by a blinding vision of the risen Christ to be asked the simple question why was he persecuting Christ. Why? The result of that conversion produced a doctrine of Christ for the Graeco-Roman world and for Judaism itself - a striking complement to St. John's interpretation. Yet in that difference is created a strikingly penetrative, evangelical interpretation of God's purpose in Christ. In his shattering, devastating and destructive conversion, he was given the task, which only he as a learned Pharisee and Rabbi could do, of persuading Judaism that they had mistaken God's temporary plan for Judaism, i.e. land, law, ethnic principles, as the final purpose of God. God's final purpose was disclosed in Christ, and that was Jewry's mission for the world. This mission was given to Paul.

b. *St. Paul's Interpretation of Christ*

Paul's dramatic experience convinced him that he had been seized by God, seized by God for God's purposes. He perceived that in the Resurrection God had vindicated Jesus as God's Messiah (Christ). Paul concluded that such divine action meant that Jesus was God in action: "God was in Christ reconciling the world to himself" (2 Cor 5.19). What Jesus did on the Cross is something only God could do. Before the Incarnation Christ was "in the form of God," but did not regard his equality with God to be used to his advantage but only to reveal more fully the true character of God by his self-abnegation, incarnation, death (Phil 2.6-8, 9-11). The resurrection is God's own affirmation that such love is God's own nature, as Christ showed, even shared with God. True, there is only one God, but in Christ he shared the deeper revelation of his true nature. Such position is not the abandonment of monotheism (as Jews and Muslims see it), but rather a tender enrichment, an advanced definition of monotheism, a Christ-shaped monotheism.

Paul relates the activity of God in creation to his activity in the re-creation of man through Christ (1 Cor 8.6; Col 1.15-20). He places Jesus alongside the Father in what are Jewish statements of monotheism over against the polytheistic views of paganism. Paul is not developing some kind of Jesus cult; he retains his Jewish monotheism. It is a kind of heightened monotheism, monotheism fortified, a Christocentric monotheism, highlighting the love of God. It was from this theology that he derived his doctrine of the Holy Spirit, at work in men and women to fulfil God's purpose in history, the giving of true life in Christ (Rom 8.1-11; 2 Cor 3.3; 6.12-18). This at once leads into his new vision of the nature and role of the people of God, the Church, to fulfil and complete Christ's ministry in the world, the whole world.

To see St Paul's Epistle to the Ephesians as an encyclical to the whole church, even to the world, rather than a letter to a particular church, suggests very profound truths to the reader; it elevates his mind to a higher level of insight. It is not dissimilar from reading Christ's words to a blind man or a dumb man. He addresses us in our blindness, in our incapacity to express ourselves. In the presence of Christ I am but a blind man begging for sight, a dumb man begging for speech.

c. *St. Paul Addresses the Universal Need*

Paul immediately begins by declaring his authority to write as an apostle of Jesus Christ, and by the will of God, and writes to the "faithful in Christ" for only those who have faith in Christ will understand his words.[1] No one church is addressed, but the universal need of all mankind, that all humanity should understand the purpose of God: that God has blessed *us*. The blessing to mankind is the manifestation they are now experiencing of the eternity of his purpose of good, and the glory of its consummation in Christ, which they have seen and experienced in their own lifetime. His language is grandiloquent and moving. He speaks of the will of God working itself out in and through Christ, in his own day, before their very eyes. He expresses it as "the mystery of his will" (Eph 1.9), "to gather up all things in him" (1.10). This is the "Divine Secret." his mission is to show "what is the plan of the mystery hidden for ages in God who created all things" (3.11). The Creator of the universe has a purpose in his Creation – "the eternal purpose that he has carried out in Christ Jesus, our Lord" (3.11). The secret of his purpose had hitherto been hidden, until Christ came to reveal it. The working out of that Secret purpose is a matter on which Paul claims the authority to speak because God has revealed it to him. The divine purpose was "hidden" or "secret" because no human being can explain or understand God's ways. It is only he who came from that divine level who explained God and his ways. Paul is dwelling in this realm, and writes from this level.

Note carefully the level at which Paul makes these staggering claims and statements. He speaks not at the level of a scholarly rabbi, but from that divine level the author is at pains to say throughout this book, that one level which explains all other levels. It is the "vertical" which explains and correlates all our human "horizontal" levels. It is the higher epistemology we begin to understand which creates a new human being, a new ontological reality that did not exist before. Only such, i.e. the faithful in Christ, can begin to grasp the profundity, the heights, and the divine power in these statements. It is crucial for the reader to be at least aware of this if he or she is to understand Paul, or Christianity, or this argument for that matter. It is equally crucial for "outsiders" (a term I use in no pejorative sense, but in a literal sense, collectively of enquirers, agnostics, atheists, half-believers - all "outside" the Christian fellowship), at least to admit the force of the argument.

d. *Christ as the Mind of God*
Paul describes his divine mission as "to gather up in one all things in Christ." He is saying that Christ is the mind of God, Christ is God's

---

[1] See p. 51, where I argue for a divine level of epistemology, i.e. Christ's natural level.

intention and purpose, and Christ is the Sum of all things in one whole. This means that Christ as the Messiah summed up all the history of his ancient people, the Jews, but to that Paul adds the truth that Christ sums up the meaning of the Universe. In Christ we have the principle of cohesion and unity. In Christ the unity of mankind is asserted and manifested. "The mystery of the Will of God" is the divine determination "to gather up in one all things in Christ." Paul is here expressing the long biblical revelation from Genesis to Christ. He is saying exactly what St. John is saying in another way and in different words. Time seems to have inured us to their meaning. They confront us like an apparition from another world. Perhaps that is what they are. Certainly Paul is claiming that he is expressing the mind of God; it is more than sound reason, it is a word from God.

e. *God's Will for Mankind*

Paul is reminding us that the purpose of the divine selection of the Jews is not simply the blessing of an ancient selected people of God, but it is the incipient blessing of the universe, the final disclosure of God's will for mankind. It is important to remind ourselves that this was no original insight of Paul, but is in keeping with the entire teaching of the Old Testament and of Christ. It is the climax of that long revelation. Abraham was called to a peculiar blessing, but at that very time it was said to him, "in you all the families of the earth shall be blessed" (Gen 12.3). There was a plan and purpose in the mind of God. We read in Ezek 36.22f., "It is not for your sake, O house of Israel, ... but for the sake of my holy name, ... and *the nations shall know* that I am the Lord." Or in the words of the Psalmist:

> God shall bless us;
> and all the ends of the earth shall fear him. (Ps 67.7)

It was the failure to admit this mission to bless the world that issued in "the Great Refusal" of Judaism to recognize Christ, a failure that Christianity in its turn repeated, is repeating, and continues to repeat. It was on his final visit to Jerusalem to complete his God–given mission to God's selected people, that on seeing the city, he burst into tears, saying how often he had sought to gather them into one, and knowing their refusal, the city would be left desolate. All who work against God do but destroy themselves. When will we ever learn?

Paul prays that the Holy Spirit will make them wise; he will come to them as the "Spirit of Wisdom" and of revelation. We echo that prayer every night, every morning of our lives. The prayer is that the

Holy Spirit will lift the veil and reveal to them the secret purpose of God. The divine secret needs a divine unveiling, as he later says (3.3), "how the mystery was made known to me by revelation … [to] enable you to perceive my understanding of the mystery of Christ," by which understanding they would know that the Gentiles are fellow heirs (that is of the promises of the Old Testament), fellow members of the body (the church of the Christian faithful) and fellow-partakers in Christ Jesus through the Gospel." By the word "church," Paul is thinking of the great fellowship of all believers, the Kingdom of heaven, not some congregation or organization. The divine illumination is not a mere intellectual activity, for Paul expressly says it begins in the heart, the seat of the emotions and the will. He uses the strange phrase "with the eyes of your heart enlightened" (1.18). Still stranger, this is exactly the feeling experienced when one discerns and appropriates the truth of Christ.[2]

Paul writes, "so that you may know." He has in mind what we may call a "threefold knowledge" which embraces all eternity and the past, the future, but more importantly, the present situation in which we live.

First, when Paul speaks of the hope of his calling he has in mind not *our* calling but the *universal calling* of God right back to the great past of eternity (as John) before the foundations of the world were made. It is this universal calling of God that we need to understand. He is not speaking of a kind of human hope for a better world. As he wrote elsewhere, "The one who is calling you is faithful, and he will do this" (1 Thess 5.24) (and "calling" is a present participle). Second, they must know the glory of their eternal future, the inheritance which God graciously gives. And third, the immensity of his power in regard to us, to those who believe, he speaks not only of God's power in the past history of Israel, not only of the inheritance in the future, but also of God's power in the present. It is in the latter, the present, where we see the truth and begin to understand the power of God in our own lives, which is the same power which effected the Incarnation, the Resurrection and the Ascension, that is at work "in those who believe." This mighty power has exalted and enthroned the Christ. Or to express this exalted majestic thinking in our own everyday language, pitiably inadequate. Christ has fulfilled in his own person the destiny

---

[2] Cf. John Wesley's expression when he first heard read to him in Aldersgate in 1738 Luther's *Preface to Romans*, "Then was my heart strangely warmed." Compare the text that forms the subtitle of this book, "A Candle of Understanding *in the heart*."

of mankind. The faithful who see and understand this truth, in his body, the Church (the Kingdom, or whatever you will) have their role in the world to fulfil and complete the mission he began. That is to say, he looks upon Christ as waiting for the Church to complete his mission and destined in the purpose of God to find completeness in the Church.

And this is where we come in. We are now living in a new *aion*, the *aion* that Christ brought into being, and we, his agents and servants, are being called to fulfil that role. In that fulfilment we begin to understand the past, from Creation to the Incarnation (see Chapter 8) and our future hope of life with God.

Paul is telling us that without the Church, the mission of Christ is incomplete and as the Church grows towards completion, the Christ grows towards completion, the Christ who in the divine purpose must be "all in all" (3.11); cf. Col 1.24, where Paul speaks of his sufferings as completing Christ's work in the Church.

Paul is arguing that the purpose of God is to gather up all things in Christ, all experiences, all sufferings, all understandings. All is not yet achieved as God purposed, the Christ is not yet all that the Divine Wisdom had determined that he shall be. Christ still waits for his completeness, his fulfilment.

This fulfilment, this completeness, God still waits for, and it is this completeness which sums up the universe, a fullness predicated of Christ as the issue of the Divine purpose. And here emerges the role of mankind in this awe-inspiring vision, "through the Church," i.e. those people who see this, understand it, believe it. Readers must be aware that we are speaking and writing virtually in a kind of transcendental language. If you sense this, you understand Paul - and Christ.

Paul is arguing (Eph 2) that God through Christ had inaugurated the fulfilment of all history through his historic people the Jews by means of the establishment of the new dispensation in Christ, whose fulfilment and end was to subsume all humanity, Jews, Christians and Gentiles alike: all mankind.

He argues that through his love (2.4), though they were spiritually dead, God had "made us alive" ("quickened" us, a lovely word in the KJV), had quickened us all as he had "quickened" Christ. By this striking word he links our new found life with what God did in Christ through the Resurrection and Ascension. He is actually telling us that a new start was made in the world's history. St Paul called it a new Creation.

He is declaring that his supreme mission under God was to proclaim Christ as the centre of a new humanity. Man was made anew by God by free grace, not by his own thinking, or by good or meritorious deeds, though, of course, he makes plain that such conversion issues in righteousness and goodness. Indeed, more, the divine purpose is not achieved apart from the good works of converted men and women. The purpose does not proceed from our good deeds and intentions, but it does lead to them, and finds its confirmation in them. Paul calls us to "remember" this, a pregnant word for a Jew, and for a Christian. One stops, and thinks, and begins to ask oneself, "Why has the Church forgotten this?" To St. Paul, this was the decisive battle in the world's history. Paul is thinking that this new vision, actually given to mankind, now actually realized in Christ, the vision of the unity of mankind, and further of the mighty hope opened up for mankind as a whole.

There is a deep pathos in Paul's language, a sense of his "last words" to his own people the Jews, to his fellow Christians, to all humanity. He speaks not the words of our so limited missiology. It is not the language of our present-day missions to Jews, or Christians, or the heathen. Not even our ecumenical language of seeking unity in the faith. All these may be justifiable in their day. Paul is caught up in an epistemological divine dimension. He speaks for God, and from God, and long before our humanity-centred views were born. Why has Christendom not "remembered"?

Paul saw all this as the fulfilment of God's purpose for humanity. This was the glorious fulfilment of the selected people, the Jews, offered by their Messiah. Why did the Jews misinterpret and misunderstand their divine vocation and take the path of exclusiveness? The Jew had nothing to lose. On the contrary, he gained everything. He gained all the rest of humanity, the whole Gentile world, as well as the fulfilment of his own religion, in that God had given him the nations for a heritage, and the ends of the earth for his possession (Ps 2.8). Yet he refused. He still refuses to see.

Further, it was all gain to the Gentile, too. He gained in finding a new brotherhood with the Jews, a place in the divine family, the great Commonwealth of God. The Gentile was now an adopted, a wanted child. Such was Paul's rapturous vision (better God's). It was the *ne plus ultra*. Yet, save for a few of our great Church Fathers, it is hardly ever taken up. We just didn't "remember." Even today, when the Chief Rabbi, Dr. Jonathan Sachs, writes a fine embracive book for Jew and Gentile alike on the dignity of difference, his own Board of Deputies compel him to withdraw the book, remove the prophetic passages they think offensive, and then re-publish it. We are back to where we always were. *Cui bono?* Nothing seems to change. Could we but open people's minds. If only they would allow themselves to be born again, born from above (Jn 3), they would see everything differently.

All such divisiveness, exclusiveness, division, hostility, separateness, Paul says, Christ had abolished in his flesh (Eph 2.15), or simply, in his humanity, his human nature, the mystery of the Incarnation. God expressed it in our own human terms of flesh and blood. To the Jews, this was utterly impossible to consider, as it is today. To the Greeks, the educated of the world, it was the height of folly, as it remains today. Yet, many saw and believed, as is the case today. The flesh of Christ means our common humanity, which he deigned to make his own. What Paul is saying is that all humanity finds its meeting point and its meaning in Christ. This is Paul's understanding of the "mystery of Christ" (3.3), that all humanity is to be "fellow heirs, members of the same body, and sharers in the promise in Christ" (3.6) and that God has called him to preach to the world the unsearchable, the unfathomable riches of Christ, and also to bring to light what the dispensation of the mystery of Christ is, the mystery which from the beginning of Creation has been hidden in God the Creator (3.8). Not indeed that Christ, the Divine purpose, is a new idea, but rather its manifestation is new and demands a new kind of understanding.

f. *Human Unbelief and Divine Grace*
St. Paul handles the problem of human unbelief and how divine grace resolves that problem in Romans 9-11.

St. Paul was to face the same hostility to the gospel as Christ faced from the High Priest and the Sanhedrin. The gospel of free grace to the penitent was in contradiction of their Holy Scriptures, as they understood them, and as history had interpreted them. To Paul, a Hebrew of the Hebrews, a renowned student of the most distinguished rabbi of the day, Gamaliel, it was particularly painful. To preach Christ's Gospel of free grace to the penitent and believing heart was simply to make the Scriptures, the Law and the Tradition otiose. Was Jewry mistaken about it? Were all the promises of no effect? Paul met this problem of the fate of Israel in Romans 9-11, the longest argument in the whole of the New Testament. He begins by speaking of the sorrow and anguish of heart it cost him in their misunderstanding of the gospel and the Incarnation in favour of the law. He concedes that all the promises had been made to Israel, but that in Christ all the promises had been fulfilled. As an historical fact, Israel had rejected Christ. Did this make the promises of no effect?

There are three main points in St. Paul's argument. First he argues that it is God who made the promises, and that God is sovereign over all. It is his choice, his selection, his purpose. It was he who had chosen Abraham, Israel not Ishmael, Jacob not Esau, Joseph not his brethren. It is to the people of faith, believers, to whom promises are made. He then says that Israel is responsible for its own rejection, for seeking salvation in the law. He goes on to say that this does not mean that the rejection is final or decisive. On the contrary, for in this very rejection, God brings about the very conditions for Israel's final, ultimate salvation. In fact, Israel's rejection means the salvation of the world.

As a Jewish scholar he knows that all the promises were made to Israel, but is asserting that in Christ all the promises were fulfilled (2 Cor 1.20). Israel had rejected Christ. Are the promises, God's promises, void? Paul argues that he who promised is God, who is sovereign. It is *God's* choice, *God's* selection, *God's* purpose, *God's* promise, which was, and is, that the promise to their forefathers was always of mercy and grace, only to be accepted in faith not by obedience to the Law or to moral achievement. Paul is saying that it is historically true that God gave his promises to Israel; these promises cannot be broken; they are fulfilled in Christ. This does not mean that God has failed. Though Israel continues to cling to the idea of being God's peculiar people in Abraham, Paul sets against man's claim the sovereignty of God. The promises were not made according to the flesh, but according to the spirit; not all Israel are of Israel. It runs through Isaac, but not Ishmael; through Jacob, but not Esau. The meaning of this is that election is by call of God, not works of man, nor by race. The promise is for spiritual Israel, i.e. those who believe.

It is vital to understand Paul's argument on the sovereignty of God as it is shown in mercy and in wrath. To the complaint that God is not just if he does not regard human works and merit, Paul does not answer by argument, but replies by saying that God is free and sovereign in his mercy. None can earn grace, none can claim it. Paul does not defend God: he *re*solves human questions by *dis*solving them. God cannot be measured by human standards. When men in enmity against God rise up against God, they think they are acting on their own autonomy, and are limiting God, defeating God. In fact, God is showing his power all the more by giving that person up to his/her own enmity. All serve God one way or another. If man calls God to the bar, he puts himself in the centre. As Luther once expressed it, "*Wir handelen nicht sondern wir werdn gehandelt.*" (It is not we who handle affairs; we are being handled.)

The issue is not what a person is or does, but what God is doing with him or her. Paul is not offering here a theodicy, a justification of God's dealings with man. To Paul, every theodicy is a blasphemy. To attempt to defend God's action is to attack him in his deity. Neither is Paul offering a philosophy of history. Paul does not solve the riddles of life; he gives a faith which puts life and all its riddles into God's hands - where they belong. Israel is rejected, but that means the salvation of the world. The scriptures he quotes, Hosea (2.23; 1.10) and Isaiah (29.16; 45.9; 64.8) support this view, and Exodus (9.16; 19.21) *et al.*

He goes on to argue that Israel's rejection is the outcome of her own Great Refusal. Righteousness by faith is offered to all the world, Jew and Gentile alike, without distinction. However much Israel seeks righteousness, she cannot *attain* it by law, for the only real righteousness is by faith. Israel has heard this message and rejected it in disobedience and unbelief. She has thereby brought about her own rejection. Paul supports this view from the Law and the Prophets.

Nevertheless Israel's rejection is not final. Israel chose law rather than faith. True. Israel is rejected. True. Is that the end? What is God doing with and about his chosen, his peculiar people? Rejected? Certainly not. There is a remnant of Israel even now not rejected. That remnant is of *God's* election, brought to faith in Christ. The faith of Israel became the salvation of the Gentiles. Therefore, rejection proves truly to be the way to Israel's salvation. It is the way God brings her back to the right. A "part" of Israel is hardened. But the remnant will become a people. All Israel will be saved and enter the Kingdom. Mercy and wrath are the two ways God meets man: he/she who will not accept mercy stands under the wrath. God's plan, through the Jews' unbelief, is to have mercy on *all*. There is no other relation to God. This is how Paul interprets the Incarnation and the consequences incurred by its rejection in unbelief.

Though Creation contains intelligences besides Man, so the secret of the divine purpose in Creation is now made known to the whole universe as the justification of the divine dealing with mankind. (The significance of this explanation by Paul of God's dealing with mankind is taken up later; see Chapter 6.)

Paul has found a satisfying philosophy of history (only part of his contribution to the understanding of Christianity). He is able to "justify the ways of God with man," he makes the very varied wisdom of

God to and for all humankind, in the way we might study a beautiful oriental carpet.

True, it could be argued that Paul is expressing opinions of his own, from his own standpoint, but it is part of the argument that Paul argues that that is precisely what he is not doing. Under God, he claims to have been given a complete philosophy of history and an explanation of the ways of God with man. He is absolutely certain he has been given the secret of the Creator, from God himself. "This mystery has been made known to me by revelation" (3.3). It is not a mere attempt to unify Jew and Gentile into some sacred commonwealth. He is thinking, living and writing in the divine dimension, in which I have argued such thoughts can alone be conceived or experienced, even judged. In this experience he is emboldened to trace the entire course of the divine dealings with man, through the ages, i.e. from Creation itself one purpose runs. Coleridge saw this when he described the Epistle to the Ephesians as "the divinest composition of man." The present author seeks to help the reader understand such thinking. A critic may find this line of thinking more than he can accept, or even understand, but such a critic may be invited to consider it a working hypothesis for the time being. He will find the hypothesis explains everything eventually. For the present study we may say that Paul is expressing the Incarnation *sub specie aeternitatis*.

Paul clarifies the issues in the Epistle to the Ephesians. He goes on to say that the divine purpose has been made clear to him, a purpose embedded in the design of Creation itself. But it was a hidden purpose, a divine secret, which can now be understood in "the mystery of Christ," a secret understood only by Christ (3.4) now revealed to the holy prophets and apostles in the Spirit (3.5), of whom Paul was one. Hitherto, people had lived and died in ignorance of the secret of their own lives and of the universe. Generations had followed generations until the time came for the disclosure of the "mystery of the Christ" (3.5). At last, it was disclosed to the apostles and prophets of the new age, and to him, Paul, the least of them all, had been entrusted this message. His task had been, in preaching the Gospel, to shed that vital light, the understanding of man's history to illuminate the past, present and future. Further, he was showing that "that is the plan of the mystery hidden for ages in God who created all things" (3.9).

Paul says that it is for this cause he bows his knees to the Father (3.14). Such kneeling is expressive of deep and grave emotion. He kneels down, head to the ground, the Eastern prostration. Normally, one stands at prayer. His prayer embraces earth and heaven. He prays

(3.16) for strengthening with power (the divine power referred to above) by the Holy Spirit in the inner being (cf. 1.18, "with the eyes of your heart enlightened"), that all mankind may understand the fullness of the divine purpose, that all mankind be strong enough to discern this and understand this (3.18). (It is in another letter written at the same time that he speaks of the indwelling of Christ in the Gentiles, as a truth that had already begun to be realized in the divine purpose [Col 1.27].)

He begs the Christian world to understand this in the way the "saints" (i.e. the believers) understand this (Col 1.26f.). The divine purpose is beyond the comprehension of any normal individual intelligence, it passes human comprehension (3.19). It is even beyond attainment.[3] But, in union with believers, we may comprehend it.

Nevertheless, inconceivable, unknowable, and incomprehensible as much of this thinking may be, paradoxically the ultimate goal claims to be the sum of all knowledge, a total and complete fulfilment of understanding. The ultimate purpose of God is to gather up all things in Christ (1.10). We are to remember that the fullness of the Deity dwells bodily in Christ, that we are fulfilled in him (Col 2.9), and we are incorporated into the communion of the saints. We are meant to share in Christ's fullness, though it all surpasses knowledge (3.19). Paul can look forward to the ultimate issue of the divine purpose for the universe, for he clearly perceives that the present contains implicitly the future, in Christ.

He begs his readers to live a quality of life worthy of this divine calling, Christ's. The divine purpose is to find its fulfilment and consummation in eternal glory with God. Members of this communion are called to proclaim and maintain the unity of man to man in the great human unity. It is not mere individual conviction and commitment, it is "to walk in the Spirit of unity," all day, all our life.

It is important to perceive how Paul moves from the realm of divine thought into the expression and realization of such thinking into our common everyday life, in which area *only* can it be *proven*. To express this in other words, we are called to out-think and out-live our pagan environment, exactly as did the Early Church and our great Church Fathers.

Clearly, in Ephesians, Paul leaves the height of justifying God's pur-

---

[3] Once again we are reminded how often Paul (and the present author) refers to the necessity of a greater epistemology, to think on this divine level, before one can begin to understand the mystery of Christ. To any but believers it is *terra incognita*.

pose in Creation (we may say that it is here he "out-thinks" his Jew-ish/Greek environment) and turns to the everyday level of our common life (we may say that it is in this field that he shows that such thinking is fulfilled as we "out-live" our environment).

He calls Christians to lead a life worthy of the calling to which they have been called, the unity of mankind: one Lord, one faith, one bap-tism, one God and Father of us all, who is above all, and through all, and in all (Eph 4). He speaks of the grace of God building up the communion, until we all attain to the unity of the faith, and the knowledge of Christ, so that we might mature into the fullness of Christ, not tossed to and fro in every wind of human thought and speculation. They are not to live in the ways of the world, but in Christ, imitators of God.

He offers a great deal of spiritual guidance as to how Christians should live. He even speaks on the practical level of everyday behav-iour, of marriage, of children, of slavery. It is not our concern here to discuss these matters. I merely point out the magisterial intellectual level at which he understands Christ (where he "out-thinks") his envi-ronment under God, and how he relates this to life ("out-lives") his environment. As far as the present is concerned, in the discussion our thoughts are directed to bringing to society a fuller awareness and un-derstanding of the significance of Christ. We are keenly sensitive to the fact that the fullness of Christ means not only understanding Christ (from God's point of view), but means "following him" (to use his own words).

After all is said, Paul powerfully and with deep emotion taught that "the people of God" were the "embodiment" of the divine purpose of the world; they were to be the witnesses to man of the unity of man-kind, one man, in one Spirit (2.15). In plain words: humanity as God would have it be, humanity as God intended it. As I write these words the terrorists in Iraq, Indonesia and the Middle East tear us all apart, millions and millions of our fellow human beings have neither water nor bread, millions riddled with disease, sightless, hopeless. Will their tears not move our hearts and reach our minds? Is our permanent ad-dress Stupidity Street? Christ wept over the blindness of Jerusalem. He weeps over the blindness of the world. God once said, Listen to him. His words still stand.

After this study of Paul's powerful and moving addresses to the whole world of the meaning of the Incarnation, we turn to our third theologian, the anonymous author of the Epistle to the Hebrews, a Jewish Christian, addressing Jews.

5

The Incarnation according to the Epistle to the Hebrews

The Christology of the Epistle to the Hebrews
Earlier in the present work in discussing the differences between the Hebraic way of thinking and the Hellenists, I offered the suggestion that the Platonic distinction between form and idea might throw a cross-light on the Incarnation in one respect, and that was in seeing Christ as the one perfect, permanent, objective reality, our one unchanging *constant* eternal point of reference, the "Idea," and Jesus the "Form." In this respect, I likened Christ to the Platonic "Idea," but only by way of illustration. It raises difficulties if pressed too far.

Nevertheless, in a not dissimilar way, the author of the Epistle to the Hebrews offers an interpretation different from John or Paul. I say different, but hasten to add that he holds the same essential faith as to Christ's divine person and genuine humanity. The special interest for us is that his distinct theological expression of the Incarnation falls after John's and Paul's writings, but before the Nicene Fathers of the fourth century had formulated Christian orthodoxy. It could give a false understanding to say that the author of Hebrews is thinking at a different level from the Ebionites or Arians. It is rather a different way. It is a kind of religious approach, almost ecclesiastical, for he betrays an awesome sense of the majesty of God, a profound experience of worship, and not unlike the "High" Anglicans of the Tractarian Movement. No doubt, in his day, as he clearly states, many of the Jewish converts were "slipping away" (Heb 2.1) from the faith, and no doubt it was to such lapsed believers he directed his thinking, and in this distinctive way. John and Paul, each in his own distinctive and authoritative way, declared that God himself had taken the initiative and drawn near to man in Jesus Christ. This was the gospel. But, to the author of Hebrews, Christ is presented as the perfect High Priest, who by the sacrifice of himself enables us to draw near to God in worship. Nevertheless, with all his sense of the utter remoteness of God in his glory and majesty, he does say with extreme simplicity that in these last days God had spoken to us by his Son.

Perhaps the author of Hebrews had come under the influence of Alexandrine Platonius (or Philo), or was directing his appeal to the lapsed Christian Jews who had come under that influence, for there are indications of that influence in the early chapters of Acts. Certainly, his language is in the Platonic mould when he speaks of the imperfect world as a shadow, as a world of shadows or images, and the perfect world is that of heavenly and spiritual realities. For the author of Hebrews, the present reality of the heavenly sphere is the realm into which Christ had returned and now exists. It was under the influence of this thought that I earlier sought to express Christ as a permanent, unchanging reality, a constant, to which to relate our thinking of the Incarnation.[1]

However, there are inconsistencies that arise in the reconciliation of Hebraic and Hellenic thought in this area. The writer does actually use the Hebraic expression of "the world to come" and is close to the Pauline idea of "the present aion" and "the aion to come." He refers at some length (Heb 11) to the faith shown by the fathers of the Old Testament. His eschatology amounts essentially to the absolute finality of the revelation in Christ (1.2; 9.28). The picture of Christ as having once for all entered the heavenly sanctuary, or of Christ our forerunner and pioneer who has opened up the way by which we are to follow him (6.20; 9.12; 2.10) means but one thing: that the theme of the Epistle is our pilgrimage to the heavenly city[2] where Christ reigns. Little we have of the Resurrection, wholly unlike John and Paul; rather, we read of Christ's passage through death into the heavenly world. Perhaps we could say that the author of Hebrews addresses himself to a particular group (of apostates?) at a particular time and place, whereas John and Paul address all mankind. His thinking in no way conflicts with Paul or John, nor with any of the New Testament writers. It is just different. It offers an original interpretation that enriches and supplements John and Paul. What is his doctrine of the Incarnation?

The Theology of the Epistle to the Hebrews
The standpoint of the author is to regard Christianity as the perfect revelation of God. This means two things: first, Christianity supersedes

---

[1] It is significant that Hebrews uses the word "anchored" (6.19) to convey this sense of something fixed and certain.

[2] Cf. Bunyan's *Pilgrim's Progress*.

and fulfils Judaism as well as all other religions, but second, it could not itself be superseded. Salvation is eternal (5.9), as well as the doctrines of redemption, inheritance, and covenant (9.12, 15; 13.20), for all these ideas have now undergone reformation. Christ's offering is described in the same terms as being "through the Holy Spirit" (9.14). The idea of the perfection and finality and abiding nature of Christianity pervades the whole Epistle, and is indeed the key to its understanding.

His interpretation of the significance of Christ is strongly supportive of Paul's interpretation (and of John's), for it is argued on wholly different grounds, namely worship. Paul sought to carry the Jewish mind-set beyond land, law, custom and tradition to the freedom in Christ, and that their history was intended by God to train them for Christ as the fulfilment in all things for all the world. Similarly, Hebrews offers the same message in terms of the framework of the Jewish tradition of worship. He seeks to take the Jewish mind-set beyond their Temple and priesthood, beyond their sacrifices, rituals and ceremonies, beyond Moses, Aaron and Joshua to Christ, their true High Priest, who would deliver them from sin and death by the perfect offering of his sin-less life. Their history had been preparatory to this end. Their role was no longer to preserve Judaism but to see that Judaism had fulfilled its purpose, and that was now fulfilled in Christ. Their previous revelations were not invalidated but superseded by God's own action in Christ. Tragically, they were to see their glorious Temple destroyed by heathen hands in AD 70, and pagan idols installed where once it stood. Today, after nearly two thousand years, they still hanker after "their" land.

The first part of the Epistle is devoted to demonstrating Christ's superiority to all other intermediaries - prophets, angels, Moses, Joshua and Aaron, but the opening verses ring out on a positive and exalted note of his divine sonship. The sonship is conceived of as unique, for Christ is heir of all things, through whom God created the world. He upholds the universe, he reflects the glory of God, and bears the stamp of his nature. The pre-existence of Christ is clearly implied. He also states, and later develops the idea that Christ, after his ministry of redemption, ascended to glory at the right hand of God.

The Incarnation of the Son receives many references: he was made a little lower than the angels (2.9) in order to taste death and suffering for everyone; he took on human nature (2.14); he was made like his brethren in every respect (2.17); and he was sympathetic to our weaknesses for he had undergone temptations (4.15). His humanity is witnessed in his agony of prayer (5.7); in his perfect obedience (5.8); in his teaching ministry (2.3); and in his endurance of hostility (12.3).

But it is the high-priestly office which is the author's unique contribution to the understanding of the Incarnation, and which dominates his thought. He draws a striking contrast between the limited, inadequate high priesthood of Aaron and the perfect high priesthood of Christ. Before justifying this statement he introduces the mysterious priesthood of Melchizedek.[3]

The author offers still more to the understanding of Christ than his heavenly high-priesthood. He writes of the superiority of Christ's atoning work in that it was final (7.27; 9.12, 28; 10.10); that the redemption he offered was eternal (9.12); and that the sacrifice he offered was himself (9.14), unlike the helpless and hapless animal victims sacrificed in the Aaronic ritual. It is in certainty and confidence that we may enter the sanctuary in the strength of such a sacrifice (10.19).

Such an argument may have little appeal to the modern mind, but it will be readily seen that it is the perfect and final argument to the long training of Israel in preparation for its Messiah. As such, Hebrews makes its own unique contribution to our understanding of Christ, as well as the understanding of the Old Testament story as the preparation of God's select people for the coming of Christ.

The author of the Epistle devotes a whole chapter to the subject of faith, though it is a different concept from that of Paul of being justified by faith in the free grace of God through Christ. But they are in no way contradictory; they address two different situations. Paul was called to make Jew and Gentile one. For Paul, the one Christ is the direct object of personal faith; for Hebrews, Christ is the fulfiller of the destiny of man. Both views are completely satisfied by the Incarnation,

---

[3] King of righteousness and king of Salem (Jerusalem?) who greeted Abraham and offered him bread and wine, blessed him in the name of God Most High, and offered him gifts (Gen 14.18ff.). In Ps 110.4, a Davidic king is proclaimed by divine oath as a "priest forever after the order of Melchizedek," by which oath David and his house became heirs to Melchizedek's dynasty of priesthood. The king so acclaimed was identified by Jesus and his contemporaries as the Davidic Messiah (Mt 12.35ff.). If Jesus is the Davidic Messiah, he must be "the priest forever after the order of Melchizedek." The writer of Hebrews develops Christ's heavenly priesthood on this basis of his superiority over Abraham and Aaron (5.6-11; 6.20-7.28), though Christ was not a priest. It is of interest to note that a fragment of the Dead Sea Scrolls (11QMelch) envisages Melchizedek as a type of heavenly redeemer and in the same manner as Hebrews sets Christ as our heavenly Redeemer. It may be of further interest that this fragment, written in Greek on the back of a papyrus roll recording a summary of Livy's *History of Rome*, was found at Oxyrhynchus, Egypt, 3rd–4th century AD:

"The history of Rome, history long dead; the history of Christ, eternally living."

and each writer recognizes the truth that the other develops. Both see Jesus Christ as the ultimate fulfilment of the promise: Paul in fulfilling the Law by the Gospel, Hebrews in reciting the long list of saints (Abel, Enoch, Noah, Abraham, Isaac, Jacob, Sarah, Joseph, Moses, all Israel, Rahab, Gideon, Barak, Jephthah, David, Samuel and the prophets, ... "words fail him") who all played their part "by faith" in the unfolding of God's promise. "But God had foreseen something better *for us.*" That was Christ. Their history explained the whole purpose of God in his dealings with man.

The Doctrine of the Incarnation in the Epistle to the Hebrews

Jesus is the eternal "Son, the reflection of God's glory, the exact imprint of God's very being" (1.2, 3) are his opening words, unique to himself, yet no writer expressed Jesus' humanity, its limitations and its sufferings in more poignant terms (5.7-9).

> In the days of his flesh, Jesus offered up prayers and supplications with loud cries and tears, to the one who was able to save him from death, and he was heard because of his reverent submission. Although he was a Son, he learned obedience through what he suffered. (Heb 5.7-9)

Christ opened up the way for us and for our salvation by his complete and total surrender of his will to the will of God. Here he is close to the "nevertheless" of Gethsemane. The surrender meant the consummation on the cross, the *self*-sacrifice of the perfect high-priest. This sacrifice fulfilled itself in the ascended and glorified Christ in heaven. This Christ makes continuous intercession for all believers, a powerful and moving view of Christ as praying for all believers (including you and me). The ascended Christ now communicates with believers and enables them to follow him. To Hebrews the blood of Christ sprinkles our consciences (4.13f.). He now speaks in terms of Old Testament symbolism (writing to lapsed Jews?), and means the life that has passed through death. The giving of life was necessary, obedient to death, for death, and only death, can exhibit and complete the perfect obedience of the life *self*-offered. Some people have difficulty in understanding how such sacrifice is related to them. It becomes meaningful if we begin to understand the language and thought form of Hebrews. The perfect purity of obedience at such cost speaks to the heart of all who know the disturbing reality of their own disobedience. The author is offering a parable for our understanding, and expresses it in Old Testament thought form: the sprinkling of the victim's blood on the people in the covenant-sacrifice of Exodus. So the sacrifice of

Christ avails for Christians, because his offered life of obedience, approved and accepted by God by his ascension into the glory of the Father of heaven, is communicated to all from that unseen world in response to their faith.

In this sense Hebrews gives new thought on the understanding of the Incarnation that to us purblind mortals is most acceptable. The thinking may not come easily to the Western mind, but to those who still think in biblical thought-forms, Hebrews does bring new light, especially on the subject of God's whole ordering of the universe, "justifying the ways of God with man."

He sees Man as destined to be the highest of all God's creatures. How? Answer: Jesus. We do not yet see everything subject to humanity; but we do behold Jesus, now crowned with glory and honour in fulfilment of his suffering and death. This means that Jesus in his humanity is *already above all*, supreme, at the right hand of God, for he endured the cross. (This is a penetrating truth to discern the supremacy of Christ, above all angels, above all else.) As he enables us to share that same obedience, we shall share his glory. The veil of mortal flesh may seem to hide God from us, but that same mortal flesh may prove the opportunity to offer our obedience; our human nature may prove to be the very means of opening heaven's gate. This is the new and living way that Hebrews offers. It is not the way of the ascetic subjection of the flesh, but a way through the flesh, through obedient acceptance of its limitations and mortality, into the inmost sanctuary of the heavenly world, which is the world to come, the coming aion. Hebrews declares this is the path Jesus opened up and dedicated for us.

On this evidence, the reader may be driven to the conclusion of the greatest theologian of modern times, Karl Barth, on Christ:

> The theologian must answer directly and without qualification, without being ashamed of his naivety, that Jesus Christ is the one and entire truth which he is shown how to think and speak. (Quoted by E. Busch, Karl Barth, SCM [1976], p.435.)

In Part I we showed how the commonalty wondered "What manner of man is this?" Jesus by his teaching led them on – for his chosen disciples, through deep spiritual revelations, to see he was God's Messiah. In Part I, we showed first how John, the beloved disciple, experienced and interpreted that revelation, and showed the mind of Christ; second, how Paul fiercely resisted that revelation, was divinely converted, and when his fellow Jews refused to believe, argued that official Judaism was stuck in its own mind-set, had refused to see their early promises had now been fulfilled, and so turned to the non-Jewish world to show that God's promises were meant for all mankind; and third, how Hebrews argued the same case on the grounds that all Jewish history had been fulfilled in Christ, the eternal High Priest.

So we now turn, after considering how the three great theologians of the New Testament expounded the Incarnation, to discuss how an incarnational understanding speaks to the modern mind. Every generation needs a fresh interpretation of the Incarnation.

But it is the Incarnation we humbly seek to expound, not ourselves.

Part III
The Incarnation Experienced

6
God's Ways with Man

Introduction

In Part III we return to where we began, Ezra's covenant experience with God, and God's promise to him.

> I will light in your heart a candle of understanding,
> which shall not be put out.

The present writer is of a generation that still remembers the value of a candle in the dark. With candle in hand, in a brass candlestick, we crept upstairs to bed; with candle in hand, we went down the orchard to the earth closet. And when the fire burnt low, to the coal-house or the stick-house for a further scuttle of coals or a few more pine logs. It nearly always blew out in the wind before we got back. To have a lighted candle forever burning in the heart, a candle that could never be put out, was the greatest promise God could make to a person - in those days. This promise was fulfilled beyond all expectation in Christ, when he, with God and the Holy Spirit, was to abide in the hearts of all believing disciples.

To speak of "justifying God's ways with man" presents real difficulties, even objections, to the mind of the reasonable critic of today.

In this chapter we shall consider how philosophers have considered these questions, and the answers they have yielded. We shall then examine how various books of the bible have considered the matter, and shall argue that it was Luther, with his christocentric mind, who found the final and complete biblical answer in the Incarnation. Finally, we shall seek to interpret these findings for the modern mind to consider.

a. *The Problems Raised by Reason*

So far we have attempted to offer what is adventurously described as a christological "Theory of Everything." We have used terminology such as the "mystery of Christ," "the purpose of God," the "unity of mankind" (all biblical, not my own), and argued that Christ explains and fulfils them all. But we have also argued that only a believer "quickened by God" can understand and appropriate the meaning of such language and the power of such thinking, for, while requiring normal, natural reason, it demands revelation, the human and the divine. It is at this point many of our best minds demur, and many plain everyday kind of people, too. They appreciate Christ and respect Christian values, but cannot go along with revelation.

At the beginning of Chapter 2, I suggested that the fundamental question we all face is God: how do I understand him, how do I stand with him, what is my relationship to him? In the text it has been argued that Christ gives the answer. Archimedes made us see everything more truly; Ptolemy helped us to see more truly; Copernicus helped us to see more truly; Galileo helped us to see more truly; Newton helped us to see more truly; Einstein helped us to see more truly. But in the field of human studies, Christ shows the whole truth fully and finally. As he was the first Word in Creation, he is the last Word in mankind's re-creation. He is the First and the Last, the alpha and the omega. To understand the meaning of the Incarnation creates an entirely new mind. One sees everything differently. An incarnational understanding has been created.

True as that is in an academic fashion, it is most readily understood at the personal level of our common life and in relation to the everyday life of home, work, and our relationship with our neighbour. Nevertheless, beyond these issues there loom the great problems of life: the problem of evil, illness, death; the problems of war, terror, crime; the mystery of our own existence, and how it will all end. These and all the many intractable problems which humanity faces today dog our footsteps and haunt our minds. The first question the ordinary person raises is: Where is God in all this turmoil? What is he doing, if anything? How can I believe in him at all in facing all these evils?

Therefore, our first task is "to justify the ways of God to men" (Milton, *Paradise Lost*, I, 22).

b. *Classical Expressions of the Problem*

Following my previous caveat that we have neither the minds nor the language to handle these ideas, I must declare another: the paradox is that only reason can persuade reason of its own inadequacy. If the reasonable reader is prepared to grant these two preconditions, we will proceed with our argument.

Before we consider what light the Incarnation throws on the subject, let us examine what reasonable men have had to say on the matter. The term for "the justification of God" is Theodicy. It goes back to von Leibniz in an essay of 1710. Leibniz was a Lutheran philosopher, a logician rather than a theologian. The term derives from two Greek words, *Theos* (God) and the root *dik* (just), i.e. the justification of God in our experience of his world. The problem received classical expression in Boethius (c. 480 - c. 522), *Si deus justus - unde malum?* (If God is righteous, whence evil?) he posed it as a philosopher rather than a theologian, but, as we shall learn below, it goes back virtually to the beginning of recorded time. Man/woman has always been acutely aware of the problem of evil. The oldest explanation, from our point of view, is Adam's disobedience in the Garden of Eden.

But let us return to the question of Boethius: If God is righteous, whence evil? his answer was: Either, God wishes to prevent evil but cannot, in which case he is just but not omnipotent. Or, he can prevent evil but does not want to, in which case he is omnipotent but not just. Kant (1724-1804) framed the question in different terms and in a more general way as the "defence of the supreme wisdom of the author of the world against the *accusation raised against it by reason*, as a result of what thwarts his purpose in the world" (own italics). The problem is not limited to the Jewish-Christian tradition but goes back to mankind's faith in some supreme power that rules the world. Any faith in a good God makes the experience of suffering and evil a problem, and conversely in a good God. In all the history of religions, and of philosophies, we find lamentations and reproaches and questions crying out for some rational explanation of "all the evils that humanity is heir to."

Leibniz formed an optimistic conception in his phrase that the world "was the best of all possible worlds." In the positive Lutheran tradition he thought it better that the world contain both good and evil, than that it should contain only good. For in that event human beings would have no freedom, but would be mere automata.

Hegel (1770-1831), a pantheist really, held that all apparent evil is but good in the making; it looks evil and feels evil to us now, for as yet its true character should be seen as good in the making; it looks

and feels evil to us now, because, as yet, its character as good is incomplete, not yet fulfilled.

c. *The General Understanding*
In rather general terms we might suggest that thinkers seem to offer
two kinds of answer:

i. The dualist conception
In simple terms this means that a good principle and an evil principle
are at work in the world, a good God and an anti-God, light and
darkness, good and evil. This way of explaining our experiences in life
can be seen in Parseeism, Manichaeism, as well as in Judaism and
Christianity (God and Satan), even in modern thinking.

ii. The monistic conception
Only the good has existence. Evil does not exist but is rather a negative good or the negation of good. It is a kind of negation of being.
This may sound like philosophic evasion, but it was held by Augustine
and certain Church Fathers, and some modern theologians, and should
not be dismissed outright. At least, it serves good one way or another,
and good shows its greater power in the negation of negation.

d. *The Biblical Tradition*
In the biblical tradition, especially in the Psalms, Job, Lamentations
and the Passion narrative, the cry goes up to heaven over and over
again, why do the evil and ungodly prosper, while the innocent and
the godly suffer? If God is faithful, why is Israel handed over to the
heathen nations? Why is Christ forsaken on the cross (Mk 15.34)?

Faith in God does yield some answers, some positive thoughts, to
which we now turn.

First, there is a kind of evil people bring upon themselves. Here I
refer to sexual diseases, to smoking, alcohol abuse and drugs. There are
the diseases society inflicts on the guiltless: industrial diseases which
miners, quarry men, and stone masons suffer; asbestos and lead workers; now nuclear power workers; accidents; pollution. Evil generates
evil consequences. Here we may include war with its grievous consequences.

Then there is the fact of sin − "the enormity of sin": selfishness,
cruelty, hatred, theft, adultery, rape, as it stalks the land wrecking
homes, breaking hearts, destroying everything in it path.

St. Paul called these consequences "the wrath of God" (Rom 1.18ff.), by which he meant God's annihilating reaction to man's sinful activity, whereby he works against man's sin, leaving stubborn sinners to themselves; he "hands them over" to the evil they create whereby they earn temporal (even eternal) punishment. This theology is clearly in Deuteronomy, Chronicles, and in St. Matthew's Gospel, as well as Paul. To this extent God is responsible for evil, though not the cause of it.

Second, there is a kind of suffering undergone only by the righteous and not by the wicked. It is the thoughtful, the good and kindly folks, who in their experience of the pain, the hurt, the evil, cry out to heaven, Why? Why? Why? Job even accuses God, but maintains faith. (St. Paul takes the view that the human being has no rights against God; his only role is one of humble acceptance. Luther took this view too, but see below.)

Third, there is the kind of suffering undergone by God himself. God takes part in the suffering of the people he has called. Through his covenant with his people Israel, God himself takes part in the persecutions, sufferings and captivities of Israel. He is the companion of the righteous in suffering. When Israel is redeemed, God redeems himself, and glorifies not only Israel but also himself. Thus Israel's conception of the fellow-suffering of God is the basis of the New Testament account of the Passion of Jesus, as it is so dramatically told in the Gospels. He is the merciful servant of God who suffers with us, acts "for us" (Luther's *pro nobis*), and, in this way, frees us from the dominion of sin. His suffering is divine suffering, redemptive suffering, and in solidarity with us. This thought finds expression in the parable of the Good Father (our miscalled Parable of the Prodigal Son in Luke 15). It may also be verified in our own experiences of everyday life as the following story illustrates.

As a precentor in one of our cathedrals, I once had the care of a choirboy who had a beautiful voice, and was of marked academic ability. Much was expected of this bright boy. I left the city and was out of touch. Some years later I returned to the same city. By chance I bumped into his mother, and enquired after her and her now grown-up son. The hurt anguish on her face and her hushed tones were eloquent. "I haven't heard from him for years." God feels like that about you and me. If only blind proud man could see and understand that the true life is a living, loving relationship with God in Christ, then all other human relationships, family, personal and social, would be equally living and loving and joyful.

e. *Luther's Biblical Resolution of the Problem*

Luther (and following him, the Reformers), were very much against all speculation (as are all evangelicals), because for them the justification of man before God was central to evangelical theology. Quite simply to them, by justifying the penitent sinner freely by grace through Christ, God himself had put things to rights:

> For by grace you have been saved through faith;
> and this is not your own doing, it is the gift of God. (Eph 2.8).

Luther's answer is a compelling answer, compelling because it is God's answer. That is enough for Luther. He does not even need to hear any more; God has revealed all he needs to know in his present state. Luther speaks of a new creation in which God's righteousness dwells. Sinner he was, but always penitent, always right with God. This brings us to his biblical interpretation and his treatment of the prophet Habakkuk and St. Paul.

Among the prophets who question God's government of the world he had created, none is more ardent than Habakkuk, who lived at the height of the Babylonian power (608 - 598 BC). He cries to God for help, protesting that the wicked surround the righteous so that justice is perverted. The Lord replies that the Chaldeans, wicked as they are, are but the instruments of his own choosing. Habakkuk then asks how long will God just look on while the faithless persecute the faithful, and then takes his stand on his watchtower and waits until he hears what God has to say about his questions.

The answer is given. So definitely, that God tells him to write it all down "to make it plain" (2.2) (for all time). God answers Habakkuk's questions thus: Though the prophet may not see the final issue, the divine justice is inexorable, and will come in its own way and in God's good time. That is how God will deal with the wicked.

As for the individual, he shall *live by faith* (Hab 2.4). The heart of the matter is that the righteous man (woman) who is faithful *to* God and his word will *live* and the unrighteous will *fail*. Admittedly, this verse applies primarily to the historical situation which Habakkuk addressed, but the verse, quite properly, has received wider application of *a sensus plenior* (Rom 1.17; Gal 1.11; Heb 10.38f.). Habakkuk is at pains to declare that this word was from God, and immediately contrasts the prophecies of the heathen (2.18-20). Their gods are but gods fashioned by themselves, and he asks, Can these give *revelation*? (Many of the prophets have asked the same thing.) The Lord is there, and as for mere humans we must keep silence before him. The victory is God's. Though all were to fail him, he concludes in magnificent poetry,

> Yet I will rejoice in the Lord
> I will exult in the God of my salvation. (3.18)

Note carefully, his last word is *salvation*.

Biblical scholars and theologians have always attached a distinctive importance to this revelation of Habakkuk, Luther in particular, and all evangelicals, in the centrality of the doctrine of justification by faith.

A little illustration may help here, for as the Chinese say, one picture is worth a million words. When I first learned to drive a car (now some sixty-odd years ago), I attended a class at what was then called Night School, to learn all about the internal combustion engine, and what was going on under the bonnet. I passed the examination. It did not make me a motor engineer, but it did give me a working knowledge of what was going on. I feel that about all I have said on theodicy. I have an understanding and some working knowledge of the mystery of my life. That's all. I quietly go on in faith, as I quietly drove the car in confidence of my partial knowledge.

f. *The Position Today*

If the Lisbon earthquake of 1755 shattered all confidence in the harmony of the world under the gracious rule of God, the twentieth century has virtually destroyed it, as so many writers testify. Two World Wars, the gulags of Russia, Auschwitz, Hiroshima, the death of God movement, and the secularization of society have created a climate of opinion which cannot take any idea of theodicy, nor even of any anthropodicy. How can one speak of God after Auschwitz? Or for that matter speak of humankind?

Nevertheless, although the question of the justification of God cannot be finally answered by us human beings, this does not mean that the question may be abandoned. It will always be with humankind as it has been from the beginning. I have but offered a working understanding in explaining Christ, particularly as John, Paul and Hebrews understood him, and also as some of our Church Fathers and Doctors, as well as modern theologians. Any theodicy of the twenty-first century must include the theology in Auschwitz: the prayers of the victims. God himself was present in their prayers and cries; as their companion in suffering he gives us hope where no more can be hoped for. The problems of theodicy remain open until all things and all people are fulfilled in Christ, and a new creation, in which God's righteousness dwells, gives the answer. The brutal, hard, inescapable, inexplicable facts of history seem to make such language and such thinking academic and remote.

The central tenet of modern process theology is that reality is a process of becoming, and that the universe is not a universe of static objects. This thinking has produced radical changes in the idea of God and the doctrine of man. It has produced many books. We cannot in this context sum up the whole theology of such a movement, founded by great thinkers and sustained by many modern, sincere theologians, but it is fair to say they raise more questions and create more problems, and leave the reader rather dissatisfied. For instance, they tend to lose touch with biblical Christianity. Their metaphysics tend to negate the biblical view of Creation and of providence. They lose the distinction between Creator and creature, and there is no sense of the God of love working in history for us man and our salvation. It is anthropology rather than theology. Its most damaging criticism is to the fact of the Incarnation and the idea of salvation. The Creation and Incarnation are inseparable. Their picture of a God struggling against evil in the hope of mastering it one day is certainly not the teaching of the New Testament. John Hick[1] posits universalism, arguing that nothing less can begin to justify all the evil which God permits in the world that he has created, permitted in the cause of mankind's soul-building (as Origen, 184-256, argued).

g. *Summing Up*

Luther argued that the whole Bible was about Christ, and, therefore, more than any other theologian he saw everything through the eyes of Christ. He dismissed all speculation on the matter as mere human cerebration, which issued in human confusion and controversy, never deeper truth about God. Dismissing all human speculation on this subject for what it may be worth, he expounded only as Christ taught and the Apostles preached. The Incarnation was God's answer. Luther looked no further. There was no further to look.

Around him he saw a fallen world where all have sinned and where all are sinners, deserving only hell and destruction. He saw a God, and knew in his heart's core, the God who so loved the world as to send his Son, the Word, into the world in human flesh to save mankind and renew the cosmos (Jn 3.16). He did this at the great cost to himself of Christ's Passion and death on the cross. This shows God's everlasting

---

[1] John Hick, *The Myth of God Incarnate*, London: SCM Press, 1977.

love. Man/woman can but respond in love and faith. A new creature is created. A complete understanding of human existence is vouchsafed for this present life, whose ultimate meaning will be explained in the reality of present experience, not only in words (Jn 3; Rom 5.9; 8.32).

As Pascal was later to express it:

> It is not through the proud action of our Reason, but through humble submission that we can truly know ourselves. (Pascal, *The Mind on Fire* (Fontana), p. 92

It is in meeting the evil of this world that God's purpose of love is shown. God enables believers as forgiven sinners (or at least begins to enable them), to meet evil in all its forms, as he did in Christ. It is in this way of facing the evil of this world that God's real purpose of love is shown in that it creates good. It creates moral and spiritual growth and new wisdom, love, help, hope to others, and a stronger faith in God in our heart (none of which was there before the evil met us). When we say meeting evil, it means that we are on a value-creating life, a strangely convincing experience. Further, it proves restorative and heartening, and creates the sense that we have experienced a deep ontological change in our very being, a new and different existence, a foretaste of eternal life, so that we may face our last enemy, death, in certain hope of victory. *Christus Victor*!

All this may appear to the critic or to the non-religious reader all too simple. But, all essential truths are simple. It is the non-essential truths which are complicated and ambiguous, and leave you with further questions. The strength of Luther is that he simply pointed the world back to Christ: all problems were ultimately resolved in and by and through Christ. He called himself a mere pathfinder. He could certainly set us on the right path again. In fact, as Luther perceived after the Incarnation, the human mind can go no further.

This non-speculative approach, with its simple biblical non-philosophical language and thought, humbly yet faithfully and confidently leaving to God his secret thoughts and ways as not our concern, convinces one of its truth in the actual events of normal life. It justifies God, and is grateful to him for what he has done in Christ to regain us. It creates in us wonder, worship, thanksgiving: a kind of certain hope. You know "with the eyes of your heart" the certainty that the final state of things will be far, far better than anything God could have achieved by taking a different way at any stage of humanity's pilgrimage to eternity.

Such thinking proves far more telling than that of any or all of the intellectuals and philosophers who have engaged themselves with this problem. Paradoxically, though humans cannot arrive at this intellectual spiritual condition by pure reason, it is a truly rational belief; it makes rational sense of all the ambiguities and problems which confront humanity. The only intellectual who really helped me to see all this afresh was Luther, who paradoxically in spite of his intellect and in total self-abnegation, pointed simply to Christ. This illustrates what is meant by an "incarnational understanding."

If you ever go to Wittenberg, study the reredos of the altar in the Town Church, Luther's parish church. You will see painted on it a picture of Luther in the pulpit of that church simply pointing with his right hand to a picture of Christ on the cross. That picture was painted by the great German artist Lucas Cranach, who sat in those very pews Sunday by Sunday to hear Luther - on Christ. The artist heard and perceived.

7

Understanding Religious Thinking

Introduction
To see and begin to understand God's ways with humankind from the point of view of God's working in coming in Christ, is to see and understand that in all our experience God is lovingly working on our behalf in and through Christ. Nothing can ever separate us from that love. Further, it is to begin to understand what it means to be a new creation in Christ.

It is to begin to understand what it means to have God and Christ come and make their abode in your heart and mind (Jn 18.28), to create and continue creating the new mind, the new heart in all the experiences of life, good things and evil things alike, that Christ will never leave us desolate, but will come to us (Jn 14.18) in the day that we know that he is in the Father and that we are in him and Christ is in us (Jn 14.20). The world cannot see or understand such language, but the believing disciple sees, knows, understands and begins his or her pilgrimage to eternity on this doctrine of Christ. We are speaking not only of Jesus of Nazareth, but also of God's Idea, God's Christ, the eternal, universal cosmic Christ, the macrocosm of all human existence, all that Incarnation means.

Our life, our joy, is to live in that free self-giving love, and to work out that "hidden purpose of God," the "mystery of Christ," in our own obscure lives. Christ will open up our minds and hearts.

a. *Integration of the Transcendental and the Temporal*
In seeking to know God and to understand his relation to humanity, it is important to remind ourselves over and over again that we cannot know by means of our thinking the reality he is, nor express by means of the language we have, that which human language is unable to express by that very language. Any communication, any relationship, any

understanding of the divine by the human is given essentially on the divine initiative; there are no ladders to heaven.

This is clear in the Old Testament where Moses and the patriarchs are addressed by God: the heavenly voice to Abraham at the sacrifice of Isaac; the case of the burning bush and Moses; the dream of the heavenly ladder by Jacob; more precisely when God spoke to the prophets who invariably claimed divine authority, "Thus said the Lord," never "my advice is," or "as I see it." And they wrote these words down, for all posterity.

> For my thoughts are not your thoughts,
> nor are you ways my ways, says the LORD. (Isa 55.8)

As Christians we believe that God created the universe of which our earth, our world, is part. In creating humanity, it is obvious from our own common sense that he endowed us with sufficient rationality to begin to understand our world and the way it works. In a sense, this gives us some knowledge of God in relation to our world in that he is rational (in our sense of the word), and purposive, for he created a beautiful, rational universe out of nothing, and us in it as rational human beings, able and increasingly able to understand this world and our place in it. To put it simply, out of nothing he created something, and set man and woman, made in his image, with a rationality, to begin to understand it all, and to tend it, and live in it happily and purposively. It seems reasonable to infer that a state of nothingness was changed into a state of meaning, significance, even purpose.

But as argued above, and as both the Old Testament and New Testament aver, we may understand our world in part, but we have neither the language nor the capacity to explain or understand God's rationality, God's ways, God's thoughts, God's activity. We penetrate into its own inherent intelligibility increasingly, but we do not have the language or the capacity to understand with our minds and on our own terms, the secret "purpose of God." But we must see that the rationality of the universe which we begin to penetrate and understand can offer no final account of itself. That answer lies solely with God. It offers a great deal, but we always find it lacks sufficiency. It still offers the rational medium through which God speaks to us and makes himself known, and most important, it is in this world he made himself known in his Word, which manifested itself in the flesh and dwelt among us.

To understand this, and receive it, demands of our understanding an epistemology beyond that of the natural human being, beyond the world of physics, chemistry, mathematics. This is not to dismiss them or despise them, but to limit them to their own field of enquiry. The beginning of an enhanced epistemology is first experienced in normal education and in cultivation of the arts, of music, poetry and literature. We cannot prove or demonstrate that a particular artist, poet or writer is better than another, but we know instinctively that he/she certainly is, and live and behave in this knowledge.

But with religion, there is a different reality, a different activity, which issues in a wholly different result, for God is involved. When your mind opens up to the reality of God, he brings into the equation the divine activity. In that moment your state of being or awareness is ontologically transformed. You become a new, a different being, deepened by a new ontology. This understanding is to begin to discover an integrative, holistic understanding of all one's thinking, all one's experience of life. To gain this is the beginning of finding an incarnational understanding. It is to discover a new harmony in your thinking and being. Because it is incarnational, it blends the human and the divine, the transcendental and the temporal.

> By grace you have been saved. And this is not your own doing;
> it is the gift of God. (Eph 2.8)
> Or:
> If anyone is in Christ, there is a new creation. (2 Cor 5.17)

This is a new being, a converted individual, who now lives in a new age, able to see and understand. He/she now stands with a foot in both worlds, one foot in the transcendent and creative world of God, the other foot in his/her own creaturely world. God is not to be thought of in any spatial or temporal sense, but is now understood by the believer as a divine immanence. The real problem is how to relate the transcendent rationality of God, independent of space and time as he is, with the rationality immanent in this world of ours.

Put simply, we could say that God himself came to show us in Christ, so that we could understand and hold together the epirounia (the heavenly truths) with the epigeia (the earthly truths), which means that the Incarnation is the beginning and end of all things, or as St. Paul put it: "God sums up all things in Christ." This means that God is related to us in our very world of experience, but at the same time maintains his living and active transcendence:

> The Father and I are one (Jn 10.30).
> Whoever has seen me has seen the Father (Jn 14.9).

Judas's question at the Last Supper: "How is that you will reveal yourself to us, and not to the world?" "Those who love me will keep my word," and "my Father and I will make our home with them" (Jn 14.22-23) Here God and Christ are conjoint. Here God and Man are conjoint. Here the temporal and the eternal world are conjoint - and explained and understood.

This whole idea of the interrelatedness of our temporal world with God's eternal transcendental world is the most difficult to explain and understand. Yet if it is perceived as manifested and exemplified in the Incarnation, all our difficulties are resolved, even dissolved. The idea of the Incarnation is not only difficult for the thoughtful layperson, but distinguished theologians may err in their understanding, and, therefore, exposition of the Christology of the Incarnation: e.g. Schleiermacher cannot accept the idea that God could be described as merciful, nor Bultmann that it makes sense to talk of the love of God for the world. Yet Christ taught both explicitly. Further, is it not wholly reasonable, to believe that if God created the world and mankind in Time, he is bound to be involved in his Creation, to be concerned for what humankind is making of it, to love it enough to recreate it, remake it in Christ? Christ said so. Otherwise, why creation? Why not just nothing at all?

The relation God established in Christ between God and man means that it is in this place and in this man Jesus where God meets humanity (i.e. you and me), in the very conditions of our human existence, and further, humanity meets God and knows him in his own divine being, in Christ and by the operation of the Holy Spirit.

If you do not see this truth and are not seized by it, you will never understand Christianity, never know Christ, but live and die a spiritual orphan. Without this experience, without the experience of this "vertical" activity, a kind of lightning from a dark sky, you will find no authentic place on earth to live in peace and grow in hope. You will never find a true meaning to life and a purpose, but will be left with your own puny thinking. To know the sheer dynamic objectivity of God delivers us from all such negative subjectivity.

We have no language to describe this adequately, this intersection of the divine world into our human world. But sometimes a human illustration floods us with life. For instance, the sense of smell can be very haunting; sometimes the smell of a flower, or a hay field, or the sea, carries us back over the years to another world (often in deep sadness). At that time two worlds intersect. Sometimes music, or an old tune, carries us, transports us totally into the world of yester year; the school song, "Forty years on," long forgotten but still there deep down in the heart. We then live utterly in two worlds, two spheres, and two modes of existence. What word meets this reality? Like W.B. Yeats, we are standing on pavements grey, but our heart, our very being is listening to the lapping of the water on the Lake Isle of Innisfree. He was actually experiencing life in two places at the same time.

We all know, even the children know, what Wordsworth is saying when, sitting in Dove Cottage "in the bliss of solitude," he muses on the striking beauty he had seen of myriads of daffodils dancing in the breeze by the lake shore, and in deep thought his "heart dances with the daffodils." The poet's mind is on two levels of thought: what he saw, and what it means to him. The scene perishes, the thought remains.

St. John is saying the same thing when he describes Jesus as being in the bosom of the Father (Jn 1.18), or speaks of himself as being in the bosom of Jesus (Jn 13.23).

This can be illustrated from the world of music. I tune up my A string on my violin from the exact A of the tuning fork. From that A string, I tune the other three, knowing immediately when they are all in tune - in tune with all the violins in the world!

Similarly, at Holy Communion we are in church, but we are at another table, with the eleven disciples; we take the bread at Christ's hands, we drink the wine at his hands, we are in Christ, Christ is in us, and in the strength of that meat we rise from that table refreshed, restored, renewed, forgiven, to go forth into the world to walk with Christ. Such thinking helps me to understand how God pierces this all too material world with divine love, divine care and concern for his creation. He does this all for us and for our salvation. We need to think and live on two levels at one and the same time.

Here I begin to understand God's meaning and purpose. Here I begin to understand Christ and why he came. Why God sent himself, so to say - as always, the right idea, the wrong language. Without this divine interference, nothing makes complete sense. What else is its meaning and purpose? As Paul expressed it, he fulfilled all things in Christ.

I am not arguing that my rather simple illustrative language is better than, or more accurate than, the plain and profound language of the theologians and philosophers. What I am saying is that neither their language, nor mine, is adequate to explain the hidden mystery of God's work in Christ. But I do offer simple examples from the everyday experience of us mortals, from music, art, poetry, whereby we do experience a wider epistemology, beyond the range of maths, physics, chemistry, public opinion, the lot, and in that larger experience make us aware of the divine, eternal, simultaneous reality, in which visions God speaks, restores, remakes, renews our previous ontological human experience and gives us a new life, a new experience, a new existence in Christ. Then both worlds, the transcendental and the immanent, the divine and human, meet, interlock into one experience - like the harmony of a major third or fifth. In short I speak of eternal life - the life God intended me to find in this life, that with him I would live eternally.

Therefore, to find any understanding of all the experiences of life which confront us in all their ambiguities, we need – in addition to the faculty of reason which we all possess – to be granted the divine dimension which as humans we do not possess, but which is a gift of God to those who know their lack. By the divine factor I mean those precious times when God interacts with the world - the world he created, and with which he has deigned to relate himself. In creating that relationship at our own personal level of experience, he creates faith:

> By grace you have been saved. And this is not your own doing;
> it is the gift of God. (Eph 2.8)

b. *The Incarnation as the Divine Constant Relates the Transcendental with the Temporal*

It was suggested in an earlier chapter (p. 51) that a fruitful way of advancing our understanding a problem is to examine it at different levels of thought, and to raise the question in a fresh terminology and vocabulary. In that context I instanced the old alchemists and the new chemists, showing how the latter shed a flood of light on an old mystery. The history of science abounds in these new discoveries. In fact, science is the fascinating correction of earlier thought.

It is not dissimilar, I argued, in understanding theology and religion. We all know that the story of the Tower of Babel is not on the same level as the words of Jeremiah or the Psalms, nor the Apocalypse on the same level as Matthew. But what do you mean by "levels of thought?" Are we back to the old three-decker universe of earth with heaven above and hell below? Not at all! Let me explain.

I have earlier referred to the Hellenistic and the Hebraic mind. To distinguish this difference is the beginning of enlightenment and understanding in religious thinking. Their difference is also clearly seen in the reflective, meditative, mystical religions of the Far East - indeed in all non-biblical religions.

It is manifestly clear from a study of the Gospels that Jesus considered himself, indeed saw himself, as the Messiah, the Christ, the final fulfilment of God's purpose for all humankind. No Greek philosopher could make such a statement. Such a statement could not be expressed in the form in which a Socrates or a Plato thought, i.e. in general truths, for all such truths are seen by thinkers of fine discernment, which good human intellects can grasp and understand. An instance of this is the idea of virtue, discussed by Socrates.

The Hebraic mind thinks utterly differently. The Hebraic mind knows that he is a mere creature, unable to explain the mind of the Creator. He knows that he has neither the mind nor the language to do so. He is but

> An infant crying in the night,
> An infant crying for the light
> And with no language but a cry. Tennyson, In Memoriam, liv

Paul expresses the perfect creative combination of these two approaches to reality when he says "by reason and revelation" (Eph 3.11). Let me explain.

The creature cannot express the mind of its Creator. Therefore it follows that the purpose of God could never be conceived by human reflection, but could only be revealed by him, revealed through and by means of historical events, where people selected by God were involved. Such historical events could only be understood by chosen servants (the prophets) upon whom the Lord had laid his hand, and whose call was to reveal and interpret such events. It is vital to see that they were not like our modern historians recording and interpreting past events (quite legitimate and acceptable), but men under the hand of God, who under God revealed God's word, his judgment on human activities, and the consequences which would follow sin and disobedience with a call to obedience. It was never their own thinking; such were described as "false prophets." It was always: "Thus saith the Lord ...." God addressed known people at a known time in understandable words spoken by his chosen servants. If God addresses you, you must answer. The Word of God revealed God's will and purpose for mankind. It is these two levels of thinking, the human and the divine, which Paul combined in his letter to the Ephesians, indeed, in all his writings. Christ did the same in his use of parables. It is the author's view that we have to learn this lesson of combining these two levels of thought, the divine and the human, before we can begin to understand the mystery of our own being, even begin to understand Christianity. This is why we turn to Paul.

To anchor faith in a permanent reality transcendental to ourselves and our own thinking, delivers its truth from all human subjectivity, from any human arbitrariness, for it binds it to a reality which is (or better who is) independently and universally true for all humankind at all times and in all places, and for all cultures.

It is this divine constancy, the divine constant, which creates and as-sures us of certainty in our own faith. It provides the grounds of our hope in its outcome, and the reassurance of God's love in our lives, in prosperity and adversity alike. It is the sheer stability of it all, the cer-tainty of it all, which creates in us eternal hope. It is a kind of certainty, a certainty more constant even than the North Star to mari-ners. It is not something you believe, rather something you know. I do not believe my children love me; I just know they do. Every generation needs an explanation, a straightforward account of the fundamentals of the Christian faith.

The first question is understanding what faith is, how to understand it at all, for our first problem is that God exists only for a person who is already in that state of existence. If the enquirer does not already exist in that realm, or at least is sensitive to it or open to it, all such questions are non-questions, all such "knowledge" is non-sense. Such an enquirer is not able to understand. Faith is a kind of anticipation in the eternal, which is the ultimate goal. Or put another way, faith is the beginning of your existence - and of mine.

We are arguing the "how?" before the "what?" How faith may be found before we learn what it is. Faith is attained only with God's help, only by revelation, i.e. only by the self-disclosure of God.

> By grace you have been saved. And this is not your own doing;
> it is the gift of God. (Eph 2.8)

The self-disclosure of God to you does not leave you as you were, as it did not leave Paul the man he was (or anybody else addressed by God). Rather, God's activity engenders an epistemological transforma-tion, which enables us, empowers us to see and understand the truth. As Saul the scholar Pharisee became Paul the missioner of Christ; as Luther, the devout monk became the devoted Reformer. On this subject Luther wrote:

> Faith is a divine work in us. It changes us, and makes us to be born anew of God (Jn 1.13); it kills the old Adam and makes altogether dif-ferent people, in heart, and spirit and mind and powers, and it brings

with it the Holy Ghost [...] And on the subject of unbelief, lack of faith, Christ calls unbelief the only sin, when he says in Jn 16.8f., "The Spirit will rebuke the world for sin, because they do not believe in me." For this reason, too, before good or bad works are done, which are the fruits, there must first be in the heart faith or unbelief, which is the root, the sap, the chief power of all sin. All that is called in the Scriptures, the head of the serpent and the old dragon, which the seed of the woman, Christ, must tread underfoot, as was promised to Adam (in Gen 3.18).

All the Scriptures preach Christ and deal with him (cf. Lk 15.27).

WML VI 450-3, 478

c. *Contemporary Difficulties with Religious Thinking*

The modern thinking man or woman who is seeking to understand the Christian faith, or even to see a meaning in their daily existence, needs to enlarge their epistemological approach to life, and in humility and penitence discover a divine ontology which creates in their very being a new and growing sense of awareness, an understanding of life, and a growing power of conviction, certainty, faith, hope.

True as this is, we have to live this life in an age and at a time that presents enormous difficulties of a social, political, intellectual, economic and cultural kind, which appear unanswerable to the genuine seeker after a true life. The liberal education we have all enjoyed for generations, bringing us knowledge, freedom and power unimaginable to our forefathers, and yielding such manifest truth to our clear advantage and profit, is nevertheless creating a kind of religious agnosticism, even secularism. Further, I am keenly aware of the intellectual difficulties which the modern reader has with the Christian faith, for I myself had a long and rigorous training in science before I studied theology.

Many people find the idea of a gospel altogether impossible. They ask, What on earth did Jesus mean when he called men and women to repent for the Kingdom of heaven was at hand, and had arrived with his presence? How could this person, eventually to die upon a cross, take away sins, let alone the world's sin? How could this man put us right with God? Or, consider the Resurrection. How can I believe that Jesus rose physically from the dead? Further, some theologians do not believe it any longer, and say so. Many preachers explain it away. And the Virgin Birth? How can an educated person believe in such a biological anomaly. Again, this is widely disputed, particularly by Protestant scholars, who are generally more critical than Catholic or Orthodox scholars, more critical than most critics outside the faith. Then there is the stubborn problem of Miracles, though on this point, it should not be overlooked that Christ's opponents acknowledged the miracles of Christ in that they argued that he was performing the miracles by the power of the Devil. Some miracles we may accept, particularly the miracles of healing soul and body, but stumbling blocks for the modern person still remain, e.g. the walking on water, or the feeding of the five thousand. What can we say to such objectors?[1]

I am about to suggest a wholly different way of looking at these real difficulties – as the chemists displaced the earlier alchemists (cf. p. 96) and as all creative scientists think and work.

Scientists bring fresh insights into the problem under investigation, as we all know, even though they often bring new problems in their train, fresh difficulties. Nevertheless, they create a deeper understanding, and live and die in this fascinating area of life and growth and further understanding. For example, the story of Archimedes' discovery of the laws of flotation (granted, it may be a little rosy) grips the minds of the young in a way that plain history does not. The reason for this is the discovery, and the fascination of seeing the deeper and truer meaning of an everyday event. Similarly Galileo, in church in Pisa, watched the verger lighting the lamps for the service and leaving them swinging, and perceived that each swing, regardless of its length, took exactly the same length of time to perform the swing. He perceived the principle that the time of the swing was inversely proportional to the square root of its length. Whence we got clocks, chronometers, the measurement of longitude, and adventurous sailors discovering continents. The story grips the mind. But it is universal. We see Dalton study lightning and marsh gas. Priestly discovering oxygen and all that followed the discovery of the atom. Of Newton in his study of light, the fall of the apple, the laws of motion. Of Faraday in his study of magnetism, imaginatively conceiving the idea of a "field force" as distinct from Newton's physical force. James Clarke Maxwell's discovery of the mathematical properties of light, which brilliant discovery prepared the way for Einstein's new understanding of light and relativity. All such discoveries, and many, many more, resolved a

---

[1] It is worth reminding critics that Christ never used such powers in an attempt to create faith. He deplored the fact that the multitudes followed him because of the miracles. "You are looking for me, not because you saw signs, but because you ate your fill of the loaves" (Jn 6.26). He came not to perform miracles, but to preach the gospel. Most miracles recorded were effected out of deep compassion for the victim, and generally done rather privately. Be that as it may, no miracle *per se* proves the truth of Christ's teaching or his divinity. His word is verified in its content.

problem by imaginatively reconsidering the problem, by imaginatively thinking of it in fresh categories at different levels of thought. That's all! Even the genius Einstein once said that a good imagination is worth ten times a good intellect. An imagination can see a problem in other terms, in new words, at different levels, even levels suggested by Christ, the greatest discoverer of all, in the greatest discovery of all time.

The discoveries of these earlier scientists fascinated me in childhood and still do. Their stories fired my young imagination and that "candle of understanding," as promised, has never gone out. I use this adventurous thinking, admittedly at third form level, to throw light on our understanding of the Christian Faith today, not only for our own personal life, but to seek to convey a truer, fuller understanding for humanity as a whole in its present intellectual climate and in all its political and social problems. As the scientists reached a deeper understanding by imaginatively re-thinking an old, difficult or erroneous hypothesis at different levels of thought, even by using a fresh vocabulary, the difficulties disappeared. Similarly at the level of religious thinking we need constantly to revise our all too human thinking by relating it to and accommodating it to the objective, permanent constancy of the Incarnation.

It could be argued that Christ is our one and only Reformer of the divine Old Covenant in that he corrected and fulfilled it. It was God's intention and purpose, clearly repeated and declared in every generation by the prophets, to create a New Covenant, and which Christ claimed to effect. To deliver the Jews from their crippling mindset of laws, diet, Sabbath, Temple, sacrifice, land and territory, to a glorious universal conception of a kingdom of all believers, the kingdom of heaven, where there is neither Jew nor Gentile, male or female, bond or free. Why have we forgotten this? Had we fully understood this and lived it, we would have had no justification for Islam, perhaps no experience of war and destruction. The Church even resisted Luther and Calvin and the sixteenth century Reformers as they recalled the world to Christ, through the Scriptures.

It is all a very sad story, as today's tragic events compel us to see, or better, teach us a truer understanding of life. To set the Church to rights is the first step to setting the world to rights, for Christ belongs to the world. The mission of the Church in each generation is to win the Church for Christ, and for such converted people of God to win the world. It may prove harder to win the Church than to win the world, as John Wesley found when addressing the Bishop of Durham in his Norman castle, to hear the Bishop say to him: "Mr Wesley, this possession of the Holy Spirit is a very horrid thing." It is certainly a most disturbing power to the establishment, but to the believing heart brings new fresh truth direct from the Divine when one listens to his Word. But above all, as Christ expressly declared, when the Spirit brings back to our remembrance all his teaching and when it leads us into the full truth (sound exegesis delivers us from all those self-appointed fanatics and spiritists), we are speaking of God's thoughts, not human thoughts.

Had we but remembered the simple principle of our sixteenth-century Reformers, *Ecclesia reformata semper reformanda*, a Church re-formed is in a permanent state of reforming itself, we would have held on to the totality, the universality, the lively authority of the Living Christ to fulfil all things. This is what Reformation theology incurs. The only Reformation we see nowadays is the destruction of our fine liturgical traditions and its evangelical theology in favour of a theology the common man is prepared to accept, and expressed in his common speech. Even the theologians of Luther's own land are foremost in this devastation.

Where then do we go from here? Certainly not under the guidance of human intellect, but under the permanent, continuous guidance and disturbance of God. *Ecclesia reformata semper reformanda*. By *Ecclesia* (the Church) I do not mean the Church as we know it and experience it empirically, but as Christ expounded and founded it, the communion of the faithful, the fellowship of the Holy Spirit, the called of God, the saints, as Paul called them. Note in passing how every one of these New Testament words has been corrupted and debased to such an extent that they are in effect meaningless, or worse, convey false doctrine, e.g. the church means a building, which use would have horrified a Peter or a Paul. We even speak of young men "going in for the church." The calling, the saints, the communion of the Holy Spirit, have all been corrupted and debased, their true meaning lost. Admittedly, the cohesion of the fellowship will express itself in some kind of organization, in some kind of building, as the book of Acts demonstrates and Paul confirms in relation to his collection of funds to support the needy and his sending of letters to teach the congregations he had established. The Church is but God's servant, a housemaid, to do the bidding and fulfil the ministry Christ inaugurated and even to complete his sufferings (Col 1.24).

We in England love our ancient churches and support them. Rightly so. We love our majestic cathedrals and their divine music.

Rightly so. And they serve the faithful well, and even the whole country on national days, and in times of sorrow, mourning and remembrance. Rightly so. If we recall what Christ meant his church to be, and what the Apostles taught, and what the Reformers sought to re-establish, we shall always remain open to the divine disturbance of God by the Holy Spirit.

We must realize that the true Church (all churches) exists in a permanent perpetual penitent state of reformation and revision, reform not as exercised by well-intentioned individuals, but reformation as demanded and directed by the Living Christ who in his love will correct and sustain us, and will send his Holy Spirit to lead us into all truth. We shall never feel lost, never be forsaken in our penitent submission to him. He will recreate us all, and we shall all, all peoples, find our ultimate fulfilment in Christ. We are thinking not at an ecumenical level, or in denominational terms, but at the level of Scripture, of God's purpose for mankind, his own creation. And, by God, if ever the world needed that dimension, that divine guidance, it is now. Without him, should he hand us over to ourselves (Rom 1.18-32), we could destroy ourselves in a single generation.

d. *Communication of Religious Thinking*

All teachers, all clergy know the problem of communicating religious and theological truths. We all know the student who lifts up his/her eyes with a twinkle and the other who just takes notes, or the man/woman in the pew who is all eyes and ears, and the other who is just there. It is partly language: the words and thought forms are beyond their range. I experience it myself when I read the review of a concert by the music critic in The Times. I loved the music and the concert, but he writes a criticism beyond my vocabulary, beyond my experience. I feel the same when I read books on modern physics or cosmology. I do not condemn such readers. I spend time in thinking and searching for examples, illustrations, parallels to help the listener see more and go on seeing, hear more and go on hearing.

How did Jesus handle this problem? In Mark 4 (Mt 12) we read of the first crisis in Jesus' ministry. Multitudes are following him, he heals the sick, preaches in the synagogue, and dismisses the Law and its ceremonial. The authorities come down from Jerusalem, condemn him, and plot to destroy him. And all he does is to tell them the parable of the Sower, followed by the Seed Growing Secretly, and of the Mustard Seed. Asked why he teaches in parables, he explains in paradoxical words, "To you has been given the mystery of the Kingdom of God, but for those outside, everything comes in parables." And then he quotes Isaiah (6.9-10, 13), who in a situation similar to Christ's spoke of those who see, but do not perceive the meaning, who hear but do not understand. Jesus wanted his hearers to see and discern for themselves the meaning of his mission and message, and not simply be told and accept it. That is why he taught in parables. On another occasion, he told them the parable of the fig tree and all the trees, and said, "Look ... see for yourselves and know" (Lk 21.29). I cannot over-emphasize the importance of Christ's method of teaching in parables - to perceive for oneself the truth; this brings certainty and conviction. You can then say: it is not simply that I believe in Christ, I just know that I believe.

This spiritual and mental progression is a most joyous experience of life. I do not refer here to the researcher or scholar, but to all men and women, young people and children alike - the people whom Jesus addressed in parables. He sought to teach them that they would see, perceive and understand for themselves - to see and go on seeing, to hear and go on hearing, to learn and go on learning, right to the end of this mortal life, even beyond.

In 1 Corinthians, Paul expressly says he did not come to bring the wisdom of the world, but that God made Jesus Christ our wisdom: "But we speak God's wisdom, secret and hidden, which God decreed before the ages for our glory" (1 Cor 2.7). And in developing Isaiah, Paul points to the fulfilment and end of this process of learning:

> What no eye has seen, nor ear heard,
> Nor the human heart conceived,
> What God has prepared for those who love him. (1 Cor 2.9)

This passage in Mark 4 has caused difficulties to many scholars and many preachers who have taken the view generally that Jesus could not have expressed such sentiments and that Mark and Matthew have confused the situations and/or the words. It is they who are confused, not Mark or Matthew.

What Jesus means by those who stand "outside" (*atso*) is that they are outside the fellowship, outside the disciples who believe and understand. Jesus spoke in parables to those not yet in the circle of those who understand. A parable is not an allegory or an enigma. The parables are all plain stories of ordinary men or women illustrating their own daily activity of farming, fishing, housekeeping, of losing money and finding it, of the beauty of a flower, of how birds live. If his hearers were to consider these and understand them, what would be revealed to them? The true mystery of the Kingdom of God is there to be discerned by any and every man, woman, child. It consists precisely in the fact that the natural and earthly, faithfully observed and truly understood, do really illustrate the heavenly and spiritual, because the single order of the divine love and reason embraces and is immanent in both. The child who stands in awe at the sight of the little tadpole and sees it grow into a little baby frog, who has beheld in wonder the beautiful markings of a mere newt at the bottom of a pond, who has handled in wonder a hedgehog, or made a daisy chain in the meadow for her brow, has already begun to experience the deep unity between the natural and the spiritual. A parable is not some story imagined to help an uncultivated mind see a spiritual truth without which aid they could perceive nothing. Rather by its truth to nature it reveals a real relation between the natural and the spiritual order; it shows the one touch of God's own nature which makes the whole world kin; and its heavenly meaning is not really grasped until it is seen also in the understanding of earth itself.

The mystery of the Kingdom in Jesus' parables is analogous to the mystery of the Incarnation. In our Lord's person there is a revelation not only of God's being but of man's, and these two revelations are inseparably one. Similarly, in his parables, the teaching about the heavenly kingdom is only intelligible because what they say about earthly things is true too (which are also God's). The true parable is not a fabrication of human cunning; it is the observation with the artist's seeing eye; and in the result, the natural symbol, or image that it expresses, is made inseparable from the spiritual truth which is expressed.

If we reflect on this contrast and the reason for it, we will soon reach a deeper insight into our Lord's real meaning when he said that to those who were "without" all things were expressed in parables that seeing they might not perceive and hearing they might not understand. His parables were the fitting, inevitable expression of his profound insight into the unity of the universe, into the natural capacity of all earthly things to throw light, each in its own measure and degree, upon the working and purposes of God. The meaning to be seen in the parable is always proportionate to the spiritual perceptiveness of the hearer's mind.

The reader will at once perceive how many of our poets could be quoted in support of this argument - Tennyson, Blake, Wordsworth, Elizabeth Barrett Browning, and Francis Thompson. I merely make the point, I do not illustrate with examples, for there is something more important to say about parables.

And that is, that the parable gives further support to the objective of this present author to find a unitary, integrative approach to our thinking in order to understand our own being and existence; to allow the poets, the artists, the musicians, the philosophers, the writers, the thinkers to stretch our impoverished epistemological thinking, too long limited to, even imprisoned by, the scientific thinking of physics, chemistry, mathematics, into that transcendent lovely world of the aesthete; and then, with eyes opened, to be prepared for the next and final step.

And that is to open yourself to the ultimate, the Kingdom of heaven. In your awareness and experience of that divine realm you will be overcome by your own inadequacy. In your painful penitence, Christ will offer total forgiveness of the past and a creation, a re-creation of yourself as a new creation. For it was he who as the Word created all things, and as the Word made flesh recreates us mortals. The Incarnation fulfils Creation. Christ offers to make of us all a new creation – the creature he meant us to be, the creature we are not.

Such is the significance of Christ, viewed as the eternal, unchanging, permanent, constant, cosmic being, the mind of God, at once the true human being and truly God.

One could add a telling example from St. John's Gospel. Indeed one could almost say that until the Last Supper St. John's Gospel is a running debate between Jesus and those who could understand neither him nor his mission and message.

For example, in John 8 we read of a long debate in the Temple with the authorities. The servants are lighting the beautiful golden lamps in the Temple court for it was the Feast of Tabernacles. Jesus claims he is the Light of the world – not just of Jewry, but the world. Jesus answers the objections to his self-witness saying he is from the world above, and that he alone among men understands who he is (Mt 11.27), and that the joint witness of Father and Son meets their own requirements of the Law. Jesus intensifies his argument: he is from the world above, his opponents are of this world and therefore cannot understand him (v. 23). To the many who did believe his preaching, he promised they would attain truth, and in that, freedom. Those who refused would live in a lie. And he concluded with those telling words:

> Why do you not understand my words (*lalia,* i.e. words, speech)?
> Because you are not able to hear my Word (*logos,* i.e. the meaning behind the words). (Jn 8.43)

8

The Church and Discipleship

So far, we have been considering the Incarnation and its message to unbelievers and half-believers, but in this chapter we turn our attention to the Church of today and all those faithful believers we all know. We have in mind all those devoted and faithful ministers and clergy, the loyal church-goers, the students who maintain Christian societies and study groups in our universities, the young men and women who care for the youth and the children, the missionaries, the thoughtful people who founded house-churches, those who pursue a Christian life in that role, professional or domestic, into which God has called them. In this connection I often think of the great prophet Elijah, pursued to the point of despair by Ahab, Jezebel and even by their clergy, confronted by God, who gives him his orders, and reminds Elijah that there are seven thousand (a holy number), who have not bowed their knee to Baal (1 Kgs 19). It is to that holy number of the still faithful to whom I humbly submit a few thoughts. In this context I make no reference to the normal daily activity of the believing man or woman, namely, prayer, Bible reading, loyalty to the Church, which may be taken for granted and are outside the scope of the present study. It should not be assumed that I ignore them. The aim of this book is to strengthen the hearts and minds of that faithful "seven thousand," those who still believe, as well as the half-believers, those who still stand "outside" the mystery of Christ, and perhaps those who find it too hard to believe. A few reflections remind us of what it means to ourselves, and to the Church, to begin all our thinking with the Incarnation, and what that might mean for our Church of today.

It is an irony of history that Luther, who sought to restore the secularized and corrupt church of his day to the original scriptural foundation of the church as the people of God, actually found himself to have divided Christendom into two (as Christ divided Jewry), divisions that endure to this day. He deplored the use of the word "church" as a building or as an institution. He emphasized the scriptural teaching of the Church as the assembly of God, always people, never a building. He deployed all the scriptural terms and meanings. The scriptural words *qahal* and *ecclesia* can only mean an assembly of people, never a building, never an institution. The messianic community, the body of Christ, the fellowship of the Holy Spirit, were all restored by Luther and the Reformers he inspired. It is scriptural teaching, and scriptural teaching alone, that will restore the longed-for desire for the unity of Christendom, even all the faiths.

a. *The Church*

We now ask ourselves how such thinking of Christ as the eternal, everlasting, universal, ever living, ever present Christ influences our understanding of the church as we know it. To begin with, it means that the believer is first and foremost a member of the universal Church of Christ, and only secondarily a member of his local congregation. The former is life-long, universal, and even eternal; the latter is a mere accident of place, or of birth.

It also means, as the New Testament clearly teaches, and as Luther plainly taught, that Abraham was his spiritual father in faith (Gen 15.6). I could say the same thing, and see the prophets and psalmists in that same light, and happily say:

> Since all are my brothers and friends,
> I say, Peace be with you. (Ps 122.8, KJV)

The Johannine theology, the Pauline theology and that of the Epistle to the Hebrews (see Part II) are supportive of the universal and eternal Christ the Saviour of the world, as the ultimate judge and authority for all Christian churches. When I go to my village church I am at that table where Christ himself dispensed the bread and wine to his faithful eleven, at one with Christ, at one with his disciples, at one with all those the world over, with all those who do this in remembrance of him. It is abhorrent to me, holding this theology, that millions of Christians should exclude other Christians from their communion because they are not holding the right prayer book in their hand.

Such a theology compels one to see that membership of the Kingdom of God implies corporate fellowship with all other churches in the world. I am speaking of something quite other than ecumenical fellowship, in which I gladly share, but of that eternal universal "kingdom of all believers." With that in place all the rest is mere common courtesy. Holding and believing such theology, we hold in our hands the unity of all Christian people, potentially all mankind.

b. *Discipleship*

Quite certainly Jesus taught his hearers to "follow" him, but he never ceased to warn them "to count the cost" of discipleship before taking up the challenge (Lk 14.28).[1] He was fully aware of that difficult road. The gate is narrow and the road is hard, and there are few who find it (Mt 7.14). And at a critical moment in his ministry, the would-be disciples surged away as deserters, for they found his teaching too hard to bear (Jn 6.66). I have always found that critics of Christianity who say the masses go to Christianity for comfort are themselves shirking the real issues, precisely for their own comfort.

I have known people who have responded to discipleship in complete self-giving to Christ, and spent their whole adult life in prayer and self-giving, working for the sick, the elderly, the lost, and for the care and education of those millions of starving children, and have all the time preached the gospel of God: love in Christ. Not that they live some grim, gaunt, ascetic, disciplined, unlovely existence. On the contrary, I find them the happiest and most fulfilled of men and women. To me they are a constant reminder of a pure discipleship.

Nevertheless, clear as Christ's teaching is on discipleship, I would hesitate to claim that the New Testament recognized no kind of Christian other than "the disciple." Many are the people who came to Christ, too feeble and frail, too poor and weak, lost and old, unable to offer any kind of discipleship, save their love. He helped all who came to him; he understood, they understood. Christ never changes.

Further, note how often Paul in his Epistles, after stating the gospel and clarifying the problems, always ends with a mighty "Therefore..." explaining what the gospel requires of his readers, what their discipleship amounts to.

For instance, consider the Epistle to the Ephesians. After explaining all about the Eternal Christ, the mystery of the gospel, God's purpose in history, how all things are fulfilled in Christ and such related themes, he ends his Epistle with these words:

> I, *therefore*, a prisoner for the Lord, beg you to lead a life worthy of the calling by which you have been called. (Eph 4.1)

He then proceeds to expound what "calling" by God means and entails. "Calling" covers the entire life. "You can no longer live as the

---

[1] *Pace* Ignatius Loyola.

Gentiles do" (4.17), but live in Christ as the truth is in Jesus (v. 21), created a new being by God (vv. 22-24). "*Therefore* ..." he goes on to explain what it means to live as a Christian neighbour (vv. 25-32). Again, the "therefore" in 5.1 calls us to live as "imitators of God," walking in love as Christ did, walking as children of light.

And lest they consider this as mere exhortation from the preacher, Paul goes into every detail of their ordinary daily life where their calling is made effective. He shows what it means for a husband and wife in marriage, that their love for one another be as Christ's for them, and that they experience in marriage that deep mystery of oneness (5.21-32). He goes into detail as to how Christian children should behave, and their parents (6.1-4); how servants should serve in "singleness of heart"; and how masters should treat their slaves and servants (6.5-9).

It is the same pattern in the Epistle to the Romans. After the mightiest theological exposition of the meaning of the Incarnation, he ends with his usual "therefore" to explain what it means for the life of discipleship, God's calling in the humdrum of life:

> I appeal to you, therefore, brothers and sisters, by the mercies of God, to present your bodies as a living sacrifice holy and accepted to God, which is your spiritual worship. Do not be conformed to this world but be transformed by the renewing of your minds, so that you may discern what is the will of God – what is good and acceptable and perfect. (Rom 12.1-2)

We cannot here sum up the profound and searching moral depths of those closing chapters of Romans covering what the Christian "calling" means in our everyday life. Paul expounds simply what it means to live a life of love to all people; how a Christian looks upon government; how a Christian lives a Christian life in a pagan society; how he will not venture more than what Christ has wrought in him, to fully preach the gospel of Christ, to bring to them the obedience of faith. Faith means obedience.

The same pattern is seen in the Epistle to the Galatians. After a mighty clarification of the Jewish Law and justification by faith in Christ alone by grace, he turns to what this means in our daily life:

> The fruit of the Spirit is love, joy, peace, patience, kindness, goodness, faithfulness, gentleness, self-control. (Gal 5.22-23)

Again, the same pattern of thought is in 1 Corinthians, where after treating doctrinal and ethical problems, he closes with the mighty hymn on love (13) and his profound chapter on death and resurrection (15). But the point has been made and we need not labour it. Quite certainly the Christian "calling" covers all kinds of discipleship including the total self-giving named above.

This teaching on discipleship and the "calling" of God was to be given emphasis by Luther and the Reformers, and finds a firm reference in the Anglican *Book of Common Prayer* of 1662 in the Catechism, where the child promises to "do his/her duty in that state of life, unto which it shall please God to call me," which means marriage, work, daily life.

We must always be aware of the divine strategy of the Incarnation, but equally aware of our role in it.

Let me recount a story from World War II. It was during the final push when the Allies were driving out the Germans from Italy. General Montgomery visited the front line and met a young soldier at an outpost. And the following conversation took place (I recount it from memory). Montgomery: "What's your name?" "Private Higgins, sir." Montgomery: "Do you know what we are doing in this engagement?" "I have an idea, sir." Monty unrolled a map, showing where the German forces were, their strength, and their manoeuvres, and where the Allies were and their plans to drive back the enemy. He then put his finger on the map, and asked the young soldier, "Do you know what's there?" "No, sir." Monty then said very simply, "Private Higgins. We depend on him."

What I am now saying is that I have sought to clarify the divine strategy for his world, based solely on the writers of the New Testament who experienced and expressed it. I now turn to us private soldiers at our outposts, who now know how much depends on us.

By way of recalling half-forgotten truths hidden within the unique event of the Incarnation, I have indicated how those who met Jesus were compelled to see in Jesus the Christ, in a long struggle of unbelief from their Jewish idea of the Messiah to God's idea in Christ. This growing perception that Jesus was Christ, God's Messiah, is strengthened in Part I by a summary of the way John, Paul and Hebrews give support to this Christology, and Part III suggests ways this incarnational understanding will bear fruit in an incarnational understanding of our common life.

But, and it is vital to emphasize this at this point, no person has the whole truth implied by the Incarnation. To say that God intended Christ for all humankind means that all who see this and understand this, that all who call themselves Christians have the commission and responsibility, even the mission, to witness and declare this in their own situation in life.

Such is the authentic biblical truth. It was in Abraham's faith in God that in him and through Israel all the nations of the earth would be blessed (Gen 12.1-5), meaning through their Messiah to come, i.e. Christ (cf. Gen 15.6). And they were blessed. This promise was clearly maintained by the prophet:

> Remember the former things of old,
> For I am God, and there is no other;
> I am God, and there is none like me [...]
> And I will accomplish all my purpose. (Isa 46.9-10)

It is no light thing to be God's servant, his messenger for all nations to reach the end of the earth. Christ assumed this office. His disciples were to be his witnesses to the ends of the earth and to the end of time (Mt 28.18-20; Acts 1.8).

The present writer is fully aware of how different from ours was the world of Christ. He lived, worked, died and fulfilled the mission God gave him in an area no bigger than the size of Yorkshire. To stand on the road to Emmaus on a silent, starry night, to stand on the sea-shore of Galilee and hear only the lake water lapping the stones, to walk silently along the via Dolorosa and think on these things, transports the pilgrim to other times when the other crowds saw and heard Christ himself. Even in the open countryside one virtually hears the weighty silence, broken only by the bleat of a lamb. Today, in that very land, the land our fathers called the Holy Land, one hears destructive missiles and rockets, guns and bombs. So different are our two worlds.

Nevertheless, though we are fully aware of the difference between the world Christ addressed and the world of today, it is of primary importance to understand Christ first, and his promise that he would guide his followers to the full truth and that he would be with them to the end of time. He would be with us, in order to fulfil the mission he had begun. It was this mission that the disciples and apostles undertook, and that we, in our own day in our own society, are to fulfil.

To fulfil that mission in our own life means to obey the call of God. It may be very simple, such as to live a good and godly life, to do an honest day's work, care for the home and family, but it will always mean, self-giving in love, sometimes even sacrifice. You may be called to bring the world from unbelief to belief. The essence of the matter is the biblical idea of "being sent," perfectly expressed in Jesus' words, "As the Father has sent me, I am sending you" (Jn 20.21).

The parallel between God sending Jesus and Jesus sending the disciples gives a perfect description of the relationship between the living eternal Christ and us in our world today. Put simply, the Church (i.e.

the whole universal community of believing men, women and young people) has a mission which encompasses everything that Christ sends his people into the world to do. It does not include everything the Church does, nor everything God does in his world.

The Church's task may embrace bearing witness "to the truth as it is in Jesus" (Eph 4.21). We may be called to remind the world and ourselves of its responsibility as steward of its resources; of our responsibility to serve and help all human beings, particularly in war and natural disasters; to see that God's justice is done in our national life; to be in ourselves a reconciled and liberating community in the midst of a corrupt, distressed and despairing world; to practise the gospel of God's unmerited grace to all mankind; to be both a sign and an agent of God's purpose in Christ to create new men and women and a new order, where peace and justice reign, and God's will prevails.

Whatever the calling, the first essential is to understand Christ, and that is the theme of this book.

> The one who calls you is faithful, and he will do this. (1 Thess 5.24)

c. *The Priesthood of All Believers*

A doctrine closely related to the doctrines of discipleship and vocation is that of the priesthood of all believers, a doctrine expounded by St. Peter, or at his direction at the time of the persecution by Nero in AD 64. He reminds these persecuted Christians that they stand in the noble line of God's people, as "a chosen race, a royal priesthood, a holy nation, God's own people ..." (1 Pet 2.9-11. Read again the whole passage). This truth was virtually forgotten right up to the Middle Ages, when Luther brought it to light. To him it meant that every Christian in the fellowship of believers had the authority, with the approval of the fellowship, to administer the sacraments and preach the word. With the current shortage of clergy, I envisage the rise, even necessity, of a new order, weightier than our present "lay reader," perhaps rather like the Order of St. John, of dedicated, educated and trained laity authorized to preach and administer the sacraments, and so strengthen the mission and message of the Church. There is no justification for putting monks and clergy, with special titles (Reverend, Right Reverend, Most Reverend *et al.*) and special clothing (dog collars – a fashion which appeared only as late as the nineteenth century, and quite unbecoming to women clergy) into a higher class, as it were, and all the rest into some lower kind of category.

9

Incarnation and Science

a. *The Incarnation and the New Physics*

Fred Hoyle, the popular mathematician and cosmologist (who in sardonic terms invented the phrase "the Big Bang"), said (in conversation), "I have always thought it curious that while most scientists claim to eschew religion, it actually dominates their thoughts more than it does the clergy."

This is certainly true in my own experience for, since Einstein, the New Physics has opened up immense possibilities for theologians[1] to find new creative insights. The scientists[2] are aware that their researches on the beginnings of the universe involve its meaning, even direction; its purpose and end; and its relationship to space and time, and eternity; and that they are plunged directly into the realm of the theologian. This is a most happy and creative development, for it is along these lines that we will discover a unitary, integrative understanding of the meaning of this universe, even of creation, and humanity's place in it (on the assumption that we will not destroy its delicate, awesome ecology, and all our research and thinking, before the century is out).[3]

Paul Davies argues[4] that in the operation of the brain there is a description in terms of physical laws at the hardware level, and an

---

[1] See for instance T.F. Torrance, *Christian Theology and Scientific Culture*, vol. I, 1969; *Space, Time and Incarnation*, 1969; *Theological Science*, 1969; *Theology in Reconstruction*, 1975; *The Ground and Grammar of Theology*, 1980; *Reality and Scientific Theology*, 1985; Arthur Peacocke, *Science and the Christian Experiment*, 1973; Francis Collins, *The Language of God*, 2006.

[2] See Stephen Hawking, *A Brief History of Time*, 1988; Richard Dawkins: *The Selfish Gene*, OUP, 1989; *The God Delusion*, 2006; Alister McGrath: *Dawkins' God: Memes and the Meaning of Life*, 2004; Paul Davies, *God and the New Physics*, Penguin, 1996; *The Mind of God*, Penguin, 1997.

[3] Martin Rees, *Our Final Century*, Heinemann, 2003.

[4] Paul Davies, *God and the New Physics*, p. 208.

equivalent, consistent description in terms of thoughts, sensations, ideas, decisions and so on, at the software level. Likewise, to say that a system has become "technologized" is not to deny the authority of physical law, but merely to use software language in describing its operation. There is no conflict then, in a universe that evolves according to well-defined laws of physics but is nevertheless subject to intelligent control. He also goes on to discuss the meaning of a natural God and a supernatural God.

He discusses science and religion in a changing world. Here he argues that the New Physics/Cosmology is now moving into the world of philosophy and religion, the area of mind, in raising the fundamental questions of existence. In this context he regrets that the life sciences (biology) are moving *back* into the area of the old physics in seeing mind as a function of matter. (Polanyi, too, is concerned about this backward trend.)

Davies sees the scientific *fact* in conflict with authoritative revelation. He discusses the meaning of Einstein's curved space/time, and space warps and time warps, and sees the Big Bang in terms of the creation. In this context he says that great religious truths, such as infinity, or creation, cannot be expressed in terms of space, time and matter, which things we glean from our everyday experience.

He asks why is there a universe at all, and whether it was created by God, and states that everything in the physical universe depends on *something outside itself* to explain itself. But the totality of physical things demands an explanation from *without*. He considers that the theological answer must be: God is a *necessary* being, without need of explanation.

He sees the two systems of reductionism and holism as equally valid and proposes a synthesis of them both. The systems are not antagonistic. It simply depends on what you want to know. It is the origin of life that presents the greatest mystery.

He proceeds to a discussion of Mind and Soul. First, he distinguishes between the mental and physical worlds. Problems arise when these interact; you may explain the brain process, but where does free will come from? Whence consciousness? We cannot locate it. What then is the mind? What is the soul? The fundamental error of dualism (a Cartesian view deeply ingrained in our thinking) is that it treats these two systems (body and soul) as two sides of the same coin, whereas they belong to two totally different categories. It is a category mistake. Mind and body are not two components to a duality, but two entirely different concepts. The mind is not a constant like π, but a living, growing reality. The brain is active but that is not the same thing as our high-level, holistic, mental world. This liberates mind from the function of the body, and leaves open the question of immortality. The mind is a holistic concept. It is timeless. It is feasible that the mind could survive the death of the brain.

On the self he argues that mind, while not a "thing," has existence as an abstract "high level" concept. The relation between mind and body is like the hardware-software structure, though they are woven together. The Quantum Theory of the 1920s had raised this problem of the relation of the observer to the external world, and must be considered in seeking an understanding of God and existence. It cuts across the traditional framework of religion, but has implications for philosophy and science. Quantum Theory blurs the distinction between subject and object, cause and effect, and thereby introduces a holistic element into our worldviews. It is against analysing the world in its parts, but understanding it in its undivided wholeness: the world is not a collection of separate *things*, rather a network of *relations*.

On the subject of time,[5] he states that the special theory of relativity argued that time is not absolute and universal. Einstein showed that time can be stretched or shrunk by motion: my time is not everybody's time. Einstein went on to generalize his theory to include the effects of gravity. The resulting general theory of relativity incorporates gravity, not as a force, but as a distortion of space/time geometry. In this theory, space/time is not "flat" but curved or warped, giving rise to both space-warps and timewarps. (This can now be tested by clocks in rockets.) All that this means is that previously time was an absolute; now it is seen as dynamical. This means a difference of how we understand "now," also memory as dividing time into past, present and future. "Now" in Mars depends on the speed of the rocket, and "now" in the universe can differ by thousands of years. Events do not "happen," they are simply "there." Yet all are aware of the passage of time. Perhaps we need two different levels of thought - a holistic approach. We have yet to understand the secret of time. Does God experience the passage of time? But to lose the traditional view of a personal God active in his world is to lose the gospel – to lose everything. The New Physics is no help in this area, nor in the matter of the free will. The New Physics opens up a new, exciting, profounder understanding, a searchlight into reality, but at the same time, lurking in the shadows, a darker world with more problems, more difficulties.

---

[5] See below on history, time and eternity.

In his quest for the fundamental structure of matter, he points to the law and order in creation, even beauty. But he notes that this law and order is both simple (e.g. the solar system) and complex (e.g. the complexity in a living creature). He asks what are the forces that hold the atom together, forces which if there were in them an infinitesimal change, creation would not have been possible.[6] he says that scientists are just at the beginning of their understanding of the forces of nature. He speaks of their understanding as at "different levels of description." This draws us inevitably into the holistic explanation, a theme of this present book.

If the universe is designed by God, then it must have a purpose, and when achieved, must have an end. Further, the different religions conceive of different ends. Again, the physicists provide the hardware, the theologians the software. This means that God could have worked by purely physical laws. In that event God would be a natural God rather than the supernatural God (i.e. the Christian God, the Creator of all life, the God of the Bible, the Creator *ex nihilo*).

Theologians may not ignore the new ideas of the New Physicists. Of all the (theoretically) possible universes, quantum physics permits the world to be created from nowhere (*creatio ex nihilo*), a creation of all possible things, including space and time. This means a creation *ex gratia* (by grace). Here we are virtually speaking of the Christian position.

Scientists and Theologians

In the course of this study, I have more than once referred to the genius of St. John in relating Creation (Gen 1) by the Word to the new creation in Christ, effected by the Incarnation, the same Word made flesh (Jn 1). We cannot over-emphasize, when considering scientific worldviews, the Christian worldview of Creation-Faith-Redemption, for it completes all enquiries.

Creation expresses the real ontological barrier between the Creator and the cosmos. This barrier was bridged in the Incarnation of his Son, all performed by the mercy and grace of God, as I sought to explain by the Christmas narratives. It takes the Incarnation to relate and link these two realities, heaven and earth, God and man, the divine and the human, the present aion, and the aion to come. And here, I again emphasize, these truths are not thought up by the present writer. They are revealed truths, distinct from and other than mere human wisdom and science.

[6] See Martin Rees, *Just Six Numbers*, 1999.

This growing understanding between the New Physicists and the theologian I consider highly significant towards the finding of a holistic and integrative understanding of man's nature and his/her place in the universe. I know of eminent scientists who have hung up their lab coats and donned the mantle of a parish priest in the Anglican church finding a complete and creative blend of the scientific mind and the Christian mind. I have in mind such world-famous scholars as John Polkinghorne and Arthur Peacocke, but there are others, too, even a fraternity of such scholars. There are academics engaged on such research both in this country and in America.[7] We are going through an exciting Renaissance.

Polkinghorne has written many articles and books towards a clearer understanding between science and religion, lectured extensively to academic societies and preached the message from the pulpit, as has Peacocke. Peacocke, after making a significant contribution to the structure of the DNA during his early career as a scientist, was called to Holy Orders in the Anglican church where he achieved recognition publicly as a leading and authoritative advocate for the proposition that the widely accepted view that science was antagonistic to religion was erroneous and outmoded. He saw the divine hand and mind in all phenomena. He proposed the theory of "critical realizm," which meant to him that science and theology both aim to depict reality, and both must submit to rigorous scrutiny. He argued that the search for intelligibility that characterizes science, and the search for meaning which characterizes theology, are two necessary strands of the human enterprise and are not opposed. He never saw Darwinism as any threat to Christianity, but, on the contrary, it offered a deeper understanding. He saw all advances in science as revelatory of God's purpose, and that all scientific propositions are consistent with religious ones. He even saw the problem of evil as necessary in this world as providing the environment for human beings to develop any real relationship with God.

All this is most encouraging for the theologian, but we may not overlook the fact that Stephen Hawking and Richard Dawkins think differently. Alister McGrath[8] has written a fine criticism of Dawkins'

---

[7] David Watt, for instance, Professor of Biomaterials Science in the University of Manchester and the world-famous Francis Collins, noted for his research on DNA. One reads of others in the journals.

[8] Alistair McGrath, *Dawkins' God*, 2004

position, a position that is positively anti-God and anti-religion, but Melvin Tinker has written a shorter and simpler criticism.[9]

Tinker argues effectively that Dawkins' views on religion, which he considers shallow, may be summed up in four statements:

a. A Darwinian worldview makes belief in God unnecessary. "Natural selection manages to explain how [organisms] came into being without there being any ultimate purpose."

b. Religion makes assertions that are grounded in faith, which represents a retreat from a rigorous evidence-based concern for truth. "[Faith] means blind trust, in the absence of evidence."[10] "Faith is the great cop out, the great excuse to evade the need to think and evaluate evidence."[11]

c. Religion offers an impoverished vision of the world. "The universe presented by organised religion is a poky little medieval universe."[12]

d. Religion leads to evil. Dawkins likens religion to a malignant virus infecting human minds. He dismisses all religious faith as "an indulgence of irrationality that is nourishing extremism, division and terror."[13]

In his brief but informed criticism of Dawkins' thinking, Tinker refutes Dawkins' analogy of religion as a mental virus. To develop this idea, Dawkins conceived of "memes," an idea parallel to "genes," which, of course, are hereditary. Dawkins understands memes as ideas or beliefs, which spread or replicate in the way genes do and infect people's minds.[14] Such an idea is manifestly illogical, an argument based on analogy. Dawkins also makes the logical blunder of explaining everything in scientific terms to the exclusion of any explanation in any other terms, a position strongly argued against in this present book with the support of many scientists, e.g. Fritjof Capra, Michael Polanyi, Gödel, *et al.* Tinker quotes Dawkins:

> We are machines built by DNA whose purpose is to make more copies of the DNA. Flowers are for the same thing as everything else in the living kingdoms, for spreading "copy me" programmes about, written in the DNA language. This is EXACTLY what we are for. We are

[9] Melvin Tinker, "Dawkins' Dilemmas," *The Briefing*, Oct. 2006, no. 337.

[10] Richard Dawkins, *The Selfish Gene*, p. 198.

[11] Richard Dawkins, *The Nullification*, vol. I, no. 8, 1994.

[12] Richard Dawkins, "A Survival Machine," in *The Third Culture*, New York, 1996, p. 85.

[13] Richard Dawkins, *The Root of All Evil*, Channel 4, January 2000.

[14] Richard Dawkins, *The Selfish Gene*, p. 102.

machines for propagating DNA, and the propagation of DNA is a self-sustaining purpose. It is every living object's sole reason for living.[15]

Dawkins is an ontological reductionist, a position condemned throughout the present book, which argues for an integrative understanding of science and theology, indeed of all culture. If Dawkins had simply written within his own field as an *a*theist, he would have received less attention, but since he writes as a popular *anti*-theist, he receives worldwide popularity. Nevertheless, for all his seeming advanced thinking, his position is reactionary and utterly outmoded and dated, even unreasonable and illogical, as many scientists maintain.[16]

Conclusion

Science has not answered the fundamental questions concerning the existence of God, the purpose of the universe, or the role of mankind in the natural and supernatural scheme. Yet science has a great deal to say about religious matters to the modern mind, particularly the nature of time, the origin of matter and life, causality and determinism. It can even alter the conceptual framework in which questions are put. Some hope for an ultimate true set of questions that will interpret "reality" in the entirety - a Theory of Everything. (In my view this will only come about when the scientists and the theologians combine and create a unitary and integrative approach together with the poets, the musicians, the aesthetes and the philosophers.) Some scientists may dismiss this as meaningless. Physics is not about truth, but about models - what we can *know* about the universe, what it *is*. Yet many scientists see beauty and order and harmony in the universe - and symmetry. Here we must see the importance of mathematics for science. This would mean that most (if not all) of nature could be deduced from *logical* inference rather than from empirical evidence. This could mean that we see that God is the ultimate *supreme holistic concept*.

Physics makes its chief contribution through reductionism. Physics cannot tackle questions such as purpose, or morality. Some people will go on thinking that science is opposed to religion, that science has swept away religion, but the New Physics is revolutionising our view of the universe and showing this outmoded view of science destructive of religion as utterly untenable. The existence of mind as an abstract,

---

[15] Richard Dawkins, "The Ultraviolet Garden", lecture no. 4 of *Growing up in the Universe.*

[16] For example, Dr Milton Wainwright of the University of Sheffield, and Professor Andy C. McIntosh of the University of Leeds, to mention only two among many.

holistic, organizational pattern, refutes the philosophy that we are all nothing but moving mounds of atoms.

Davies claims that he began his studies by making the claim that science offers a surer path than religion in the search of God, but concludes that only by understanding the world in its many aspects - reductionist and holistic, mathematical and poetic, through forces, fields and particles, as well as through good and evil - that we will come to understand ourselves, and the meaning behind this universe, our home.

b. *Christ: The Theologians' "Theory of Everything"*
What we are saying is that the New Physicists are seeking what they call "A Theory of Everything," a formula that would explain all life and human existence, everything.

They speak of some super-unified theory involving a super-symmetry, its goal the compelling dream of a unified field theory; a single field of force that incorporates within it all the forces of nature: gravity, electromagnetism, and the two nuclear forces; a superunified theory which would yield a complete description of the universe; a magnificent mathematical theory that will encompass all of physics (in the reductionist sense) in one super law as Paul Davies expresses it.[17] Stephen Hawking claims that to discover the "Theory of Everything" would reveal the mind of God.

And fascinating are their discoveries as they open up new horizons and publish their findings. To read of how they arrived at the theory of the Big Bang; to read of how their telescopes reveal now before our very eyes the actual creation of new stars, and events which happened millions of years ago; to read the works of Paul Davies, for example, still better to hear him lecture, as he raises the question of man's creation, cosmological questions on the meaning of existence, the purpose of life; all this signifies that the New Physics is now treading on the grounds of the theologians and encroaching on their fields of enquiry. They are seeking a new "Theory of Everything" which will hold all known knowledge in a single formula. This is good news indeed. Most exciting. For it indicates that no longer can the scientist yield the full truth of human existence. Naturally, his/her expertise will confine him/her to the fields of Physics, Mathematics and Chemistry, i.e. to Matter, but for scientific theory to reach completion, it requires the thinking of the theologian. Scientists and theologians are thinking and

---

[17] Paul Davies, *God and the New Physics*, p. 216.

working to this end, and the significance of this intellectual movement is argued in Chapter 10.

Roger Penrose, in a recent massive and imaginative work, backed by equations and brilliant didactic diagrams,[18] concludes that we still have a long way to go before we have a viable "theory of everything" (in scientific terminology, of course). But as we suggested earlier,[19] he does propose a Platonic reality to mathematics, as St. Augustine did, that mathematics exists in an abstract sense independent of the human mind, and that the mathematical mind discovers reality and does not invent it. He recognizes three levels of "world" in our thinking, or three different kinds of existence (a view argued in this book in a different terminology).[20] He argues that we must recognize these three different kinds of "world" as representing three different forms of existence - the physical, the mental and the mathematical. He still finds the "theory of everything" elusive. Will an incarnational understanding suggest a creative fusion, an intelligent integration, a "road to reality"?

It should be remembered that when scientists speak of a "Theory of Everything," their "everything" is limited to what they can see, feel, handle, define, formulate mathematically. Rightly so. On the other hand, the theologian's "theory of everything" means precisely what it says, "everything," the total experience of humankind. The scientist *qua* scientist can but create his/her own world of meaning, which is extremely interesting in itself, and which we respect; the theologian opens up the meaning revealed by Christ. One can almost say that in studying modern physics, modern cosmology, and modern atomic theory, in the very moment the physicists try to explain "everything," "everything" in the normal full sense of the word, they find themselves in the world of the theologian and the philosopher. The theologian requests the scientist to give due thought to this phenomenon. The physicist is studying the notes, the theologian is listening to the music; why not sit down together to study and listen, perhaps to hear?

For two hundred and fifty years, scientific thinking has sought to remove the divine aura from Jesus. Science seems to have emptied the universe of absolutes and left us commonalty with the barren and divisive world of human autonomy. The regrettable fact in this otherwise

---

[18] Roger Penrose: *The Road to Reality: A Complete Guide to the Laws of the Universe*, Vintage, 2005.

[19] Cf. Chapter 7.

[20] Cf. Chapter 7.

beneficial movement of thought, to the present writer, is that too many biblical scholars and theologians swim with the tide, and offer to questing mankind only what the scientist offers in more exact language.

The unique contribution the theologian makes in this vital debate is to declare that in Christ God was his *own* Apostle. Christ is his mind. Jesus, the Word in flesh, spoke the word of God.

To science, now engaged in questions such as: How did the world begin? How will it end? and claiming to be on the verge of offering a surer path to God than can religion, Theology (long concerned with such questions) claims to offer the one single, certain, final divine clue to the riddle of Creation, namely Jesus Christ. This is the sole concern of this present study.

How the world gradually saw that the historic Jesus was the eternal, universal, cosmic Christ, God's own Apostle, is indicated in Parts I and II. I am bold enough to suggest in Part III some broad lines as to what this means for our present-day world. I am perfectly aware that all such themes as the Incarnation, the mystery of Christ, the purpose of God in Creation and in history, the mystery of his will, the hiddenness of God (all themes of the New Testament, all handled in this book), will only become fully apparent in the fullness of time, as Christ and the New Testament writers plainly taught.

The present book seeks to show that some theologians are deeply aware of this creative development. There is strong hope of a *rapprochement* of the New Physicists with certain far-seeing theologians. In the next few years the present author foresees the culmination of the work and thinking of such physicists and theologians breaking through into a glorious Second Renaissance, perhaps more significant than the Renaissance/Reformation of the fifteenth and sixteenth centuries which sought to restore the old order rather than create a new, and a far more productive one, in that it will convince both the scientific world and the religious and theological world together, and carry humankind into a new world of understanding.

These two activities of science and theology are seen by the general populace as mutually exclusive, but by those scholars thinking and researching in these areas, this is all past, and they consider we are on the brink of a great breakthrough (assuming we do not destroy ourselves). In that breakthrough the present author believes that the key to this new understanding will be found in a fresh understanding of the Christ Event, in the linking of the Creation with the Incarnation: the Creation of everything and the New Creation of humankind in and through Christ. "See, I am making all things new" (Rev 21.5). We are not engaged in any scientific enquiry, but only in a deeper understanding of Christ. We see Christ as the theologian's Theory of Everything, the completion of the human quest for meaning.

As the New Physicists are driven into the traditional fields of religion and theological enquiry by the sheer logic of their enquiry, I am suggesting that the sheer flesh and blood of the Incarnation sheds a divine light on the thinking and researches of our frail and finite mortal minds. Christ, in his explanation of our normal life, covered all these themes of creation, time and eternity, history, the end or goal of all history, not as the scientists think (quite properly) but as God's own Apostle, for he claimed that all his teaching was from God, that he had been sent from God to lead mankind into the whole truth.

The Incarnation, in its sheer perfect humanity, was able to take our humanity into the realm of the divine. Jesus effected this, not by high learning or human cerebration, but very simply *showing* to those unsophisticated listeners how to discern, beyond their humdrum life of fishing and farming and housekeeping, the deep divine nature of human existence and its ultimate goal. This he did mainly by parables for the people, though with profounder development for his disciples. He led them from the world they knew to the divine meaning of that world (as we have argued in Chapter 3).

c. *The Incarnation and History, Time, Eternity*

Christ's use of parable as a means of elevating the natural earth-bound mind of man to an awareness of God, moves the argument to a similar transition in our understanding of history and time, and therefore of eternity.

Christ showed that the natural world, in which we all live and of which we all have at least a partial understanding, will, if properly understood, lead us to the spiritual world. The reason behind this is that God created the universe, including mankind, and his hand and his mind may be partially detected by every soul if he/she will only look and perceive, hear and understand. It is a wholly delightful and joyous way of discovering truth for and by oneself, and of growing in it in time, of which history is the story, and whose ultimate and final explanation is Christ, who fulfils all things.

Such parabolic thinking further creates a unitary, integrative thinking, which in turn produces an extended epistemology capable of conceiving the spiritual dimension, ultimately God and Christ.

I have just referred to Jesus' use of parable to stir "the people of the land" to a larger awareness and a deeper knowledge of their common earthly experience, to lead them from earth to heaven, to see for themselves, rather than simply to be told it. But there is a further point to be made.

It must be obvious to the thoughtful reader that poets, artists and musicians do precisely the same in their own medium. William Blake "saw heaven in a wild flower" (as Jesus did). E.B. Browning's "earth was crammed with heaven." Mozart and Beethoven raise us to an awareness far beyond our own capacity to conceive or create. Vincent van Gogh, the failed evangelist to those desperately poor, turned to art, and in so doing, founded modern art, leaving paintings that carry us from earth to heaven. And this is precisely how we educate our students and teach our own children: to help them to see more and go on seeing, to hear more and go on hearing, to learn more and go on learning on their own.

Let us then turn to the subject of human history in time, to seek to know its meaning, purpose, and end, and learn what the temporal Christ saw, and what the eternal Christ has to say to us now.

We spoke earlier of the prophetic interpretation of history, and indeed of all the Old Testament writers, of a purposive account of God dealing with humanity in time (history), the purpose being "for us and for our salvation." Christ stood in this direct line. His first words were that the time was fulfilled in him. The kingdom of God was at hand: repent and believe the gospel (Mk 1.14-18).

I am fully aware that to many historians, whether they be atheists or agnostics, as well as to the many who do not think on these things, that such statements and assertions are to them meaningless and unverifiable, indeed nonsense. Therefore, further explanation is demanded, and some answer to the questions the critics raise: e.g. how can a God who exists in eternity relate to a humankind living in real normal time, as day succeeds to day? They may say that as far as they are concerned, life is "just one damned thing after another." That is true enough. All too true for far too many. Some are in difficulties over the problems of evil; they ask how a good God could permit all the evil and horrors that make up our everyday life. The need to consider the Christian response has never been more urgent than it is today. The religious and Christian understanding goes by default. Millions listen to Christ in church and chapel, in school and university, but they are like the people whom Christ himself addressed and whom he described as "standing without," hearing but not perceiving, seeing but not understanding. All too often they think of him as the itinerant preacher, powerful in truth but an impractical idealist, a kind of pure socialist, a dreamer. But as God Incarnate? They come under the criticism Luther levelled against Erasmus in his book *On the Freedom of the Will* (1524): "Your God is too human."

The fact is, unless we understand Christ in the terms he described himself and in the terms the disciples and apostles explained his uniqueness; unless we experience the humbling conversion, and live and think and do everything in this new ontological transformation, we shall never know, never understand Christ, but shall live in a lie, and die in a lie - as Christ said to the Jews in their very Temple, "You are living a lie and will die in a lie" (Jn 8.44). We shall never know the deep mystery of Christ, whence he came, why he came, and where he went; neither shall we ever know or understand what John, Paul, the author of Hebrews and the other New Testament writers wrote from hearts that burned within them; we shall never know the true meaning of life in our own existential experiences, nor know the secret purpose of God which Paul sought so earnestly to expound in his closing days to both Christians and Jews, above all to pagans and Gentiles, really to all humankind for all time.

Just as any historian studying a period or a theme could deduce from the facts all the preceding facts responsible for the situation he/she is examining, and similarly, just as a scientist could deduce from a series of natural changes the causes of those changes on the Newtonian principle of Cause and Effect, so similarly the theologian finds in the fact of his/her own conversion, that the entire sacred history, the historians, the prophets, the poets and the theologians of the Bible all thought on these lines. They perceived and understood the meaning in and beyond the events themselves. They all perceived that Israel's faith is based on the ever-renewed facts of its history - the call of Abraham and of Moses, the deliverance from bondage in Egypt, from slavery in Babylon, back to their promised Land. What is the purpose of this restoration?

In our own times Rudolf Bultmann (1884-1976) has put another interpretation on this biblical redemptive history. He argues that the historical basis of the Christian gospel is not accessible to the historian. He sees the gospel as a bare announcement of the coming of Christ, a challenge to the hearer to respond to the possibility of authentic existence by making him/herself open to the future. This demythologized version of the gospel appealed to the post-war students of Germany, who used to argue that it conserved the gospel in its emphasis on justification by faith alone in Christ, who is God's word of grace to sinful man. Whenever and wherever he preached, he packed the churches (the present author was then a student there). I felt at the time that a gospel not ingredient in the facts of history and in the words of history was no gospel at all, but a mere idea.

Oscar Cullmann (New Testament scholar) in his perceptive book, *Christ and Time* (1956, 1962), argued to restore "revelatory history" (as against Bultmann), saying, "... all revelation is God's love as redemptive history is the heart of New Testament theology." G.E. Ladd has made a notable attempt to maintain Cullmann's view.[21]

Karl Barth has always maintained a dynamic rather than a static conceptual view. God's transcendence is not his absolute otherness in relation to time and space. He emphasized God's freedom to be immanent to humanity in time and space. He did not conceive of eternity negatively as God's timelessness, but positively as God's time, his authentic temporality. This authentic temporality is distinguished from human time not merely by its duration (in contrast to Cullmann) but by what Barth defines as its pure simultaneity. God is not dominated by the succession and division of past, present and future, but possesses time in that pure simultaneity in which past, present and future coinhere without the blurring of the distinction between them. God's constancy does not consist in some abstract immutability, but in his faithfulness *in time as the living God*. This authentic time of God is the prototype and source of humanly perceived time, and in Jesus Christ, this true time has occurred amidst fallen time as the fulfilment of time. God's eternity is real time in contrast to unreal time or fallen human time; God has time, we only experience time in the fleetingness of its distinctions.

Boethius (c. 480 - 524) defined eternity as *interminabilis vitae tota simul et perfecta possessio* (the total simultaneous and complete possession of unlimited life). He expresses the eternity of the living God who possesses life in freedom, in harmony with Hebraic thinking as distinct from abstract Hellenistic thinking and terminology.

Hellenistic thinking, and philosophy in general are utterly foreign to the faith in the living God of the Bible, who in the fullness of time (which means God's chosen moment), and of pure love, sent Christ "for us and for our salvation," and by "us" we mean as Christ (and all the New Testament writers) expressed it, all humankind the world over.

---

[21] G.E. Ladd, *Theology of the New Testament*, 1974.

A very distinguished cellist once told the following story. He had a very brilliant pupil who was a striking performer, a promising virtuoso. Yet, as the teacher listened to his pupil's performance, he felt the young man's playing "lacked something," a deficiency the teacher found hard to express, and therefore difficult to rectify. As the teacher reflected on this, he asked his pupil one day what was in his mind as he played a particularly difficult passage. The pupil, who displayed a brilliant mastery of the technique of playing the cello, replied that it was the technique of playing these difficult passages. At once the teacher perceived the deficiency. His prime thought was his own playing, his technique, not the music he was playing. In fact, he never understood what the composer was saying, never heard, never understood the composer and his music. He played the notes, not the music. He was but a brilliant technician and performer. He stood "outside," like all the crowds who heard Christ, who saw but did not perceive, who heard but did not understand (Mk 4.12). There is more to music than the scraping of a horsehair bow on a stretched string, even if brilliantly performed. There is more to time than clocks and figures on a dial.

The whole argument of this book is that the Incarnation, the complete and ultimate revelation, understood as Christ himself explained it, as given him by God, yields a complete explanation of human existence, and further, will yield a "Theory of Everything" to make all knowledge cohere. Therefore I repeat the words of the divine voice on the Incarnation given at these special moments of revelation, "This is my beloved son. Listen to him."

Related to the theme of science and religion, though this may not at first be obvious, I add a simple postscript. Many people have been impressed and moved by the vigour and liveliness and the evangelical fervour of the church life of the Afro-West Indian congregations shown on television, as well as reports on the growth of West African Christianity. Many speak of this as the growth area of Christian Faith, and world-renowned missiologists are giving close attention to this phenomenon of the religious fervour of the global south in relation to the West, and even speak of a New Christendom coming to birth before our very eyes.

Further, and this point is germane to the present book: whatever the developments from the cultures and religions of the global south, they will not and cannot meet the contemporary challenge to Christianity of modern science. Science originated in Western Christendom. Its developments permeate all culture, all religions, all civilizations the world over. The challenge of science to all religious thinking which is now worldwide, cannot be met at an appropriate level by any kind of religious enthusiasm, but only by the disciplined, informed critical faculties of the educated theological West; at that level and only at that level.

In a recent book[22] Dr. Timothy Yates, a reputable missiologist, has compiled a group of papers written by scholarly, ecumenically minded missiologists on the nature and structure of the emerging New Christendom. The scholars from all over the world met in Belfast to confer on the significance of the book, *The Next Christendom*, by Philip Jenkins (2002). Jenkins has forecast large demographic growth of Christians in the global south, and asks how African, Asian and Oceanic Christianity will relate to World Islam. Among other issues he raises the question of the possibility of Holy War arising as the world confronts new religious realities and new faith groupings. This would be an unmitigated disaster for us all. All Christians must do their utmost to reject any such confrontation. We "speak the truth in love" (Eph 4.15).

Be that as it may, the present author warns against any cultural, even fashionable, interpretations of Christianity originating in Africa, South East Asia or South America. We are not persuaded by numbers, only by truth. Speaking as an Anglican, we have the three-fold formula of Scripture, Tradition and Reason to guide us. Whatever developments occur in the future, all must be assessed in the following manner: first in the light of critical biblical scholarship; second, in the light of our mighty catholic tradition of our great Latin Fathers (Irenaeus, Tertullian, Cyprian, Augustine) and the Greek Fathers (Clement, Origen, the Cappadocian Fathers, Chrysostom), and by our Nicene and Chalcedonian Fathers; and third, in the light of sound reason. We do not ask for blind faith, but informed, reasonable and rational understanding.

All ideas of the New Christendom, however, must submit to and be judged by these three criteria, no matter how numerous or how popular they may become. So-called "Western Christendom" has preserved these principles, and we in the West must maintain them.

d. *"The Language of God"*

In this chapter on the New Physicists and theological science, I have said that the scientists and theologians had bumped into one another in their researches, and that this development augured well for a future

---

[22] Timothy Yates, ed., *Mission and the Next Christendom*, 2005.

harmony between science and religion. In this chapter I also argued that a full understanding of the Incarnation would prove to be the cement that would bind the scientific understanding and the theological understanding together. Since writing the chapter, Francis Collins, the head of the American Genome Project, has published a fascinating account of the findings of this group of scientists. The discovery of the human genome must be the greatest and the most consequential of all human discoveries. Aghast at its wonder and its potential significance, Bill Clinton exclaimed in wonder, "It is the language of God!" And so Francis Collins named his book.

That research stands for itself, for all time. But I seek a further significance in relating that pioneer book to this present book, for Collins gives a moving account of how his researches drove him by the sheer logic of the discoveries from a scientific atheism to total commitment to the Christian faith. In no sense does he seek to evangelize, but expresses his thinking as a trained scientist examining the evidence in a highly critical and objective manner.

He began his scientific career at Yale, where he completed his postgraduate studies. Not convinced that his future lay in university teaching, he entered the medical school, where his life took on a profounder meaning. Closely related to patients in their sufferings, sicknesses and problems, he was deeply moved by the sheer complexities of humankind. He began to ask what was the meaning of life, if any. It was when he discovered the sheer complexity of the human genome sequence, and the displacement or mutation of one gene among the millions in the human cell, that he broke through.

He further discovered that the slightest irregularity in the arrangement of the numbers in the DNA code[23] produced grave disorders, such as cystic fibrosis, so delicately and finely is the human self-tuned, that he broke into a new awareness; he experienced a new birth. Music only, and only music has the same effect on the human spirit. It is worthy of note that Collins is a musician.

The world knows the meaning and potential of the discovery of the double helix by this team, and other scientists are already at work in this field. The reader may find the real account in the appropriate journals and textbooks. My concern here is to relate this to the present book.

---

[23] DNA: *deoxyribonucleic* acid. Molecule found in cells of all living things, which contains the unique genetic code that makes individuals different from each other, but similar to parents and same species. DNA is found in the *chromosomes* in the cell nucleus. It is two long chains of organic compounds called *nucleotides*, joined together in a double helix structure.

In his book[24] he deplores the great chasm that now exists between science and religion. He then turns to examine the great problems of human existence: the origin of the universe, life on earth, covering man, microbes, and animals. This brings him to his researches on the human genome sequence, and the astounding discovery of the double helix sequence (the language of God).

It is in light of this research that he argues that there are four possible ways of relating science and faith. The first option is that of atheism or agnosticism. The second option is that of Creationism, which as a Darwinian he finds untenable. The third option is what is called Intelligent Design, which he considers unscientific. The fourth option he names *Biologos*, by which he means science and faith in harmony in different terminology. This is in no way a summary of Collins's valuable book. Collins's work is quoted because it supports, even fulfils, the theme of the present study, and at the highest international scientific level.

It was the factual discovery of the human genome sequence that compelled him to think again, and to think further. When he began to fathom the reality that every cell in the human body, which was made up of millions and millions of them, and that their individual structure was unique to each and every individual on earth - our DNA - he, and we, became aware of the majesty and meaning of such facts. Like the Psalmist, centuries ago, gazing up at those wonderful night skies of Arabia, who wrote:

> When I consider the heavens, the work of thine hands,
> What is man, that thou art mindful of him?
> And the son of man, that thou visitest him? (Ps 8.3, 4, KJV)

The microcosm affects us as deeply as the macrocosm.

What then do we deduce from these facts? Surely it is to take Collins's Option Four: theistic evolution. *Biologos*.

★ ★ ★ ★ ★ ★

Post Scriptum

The manuscript of the present book was completed in the late summer of 2006, when the Noble Lectures of Owen Gingerich appeared (*God's Universe*, 2006). These weighty and important lectures by the distinguished Harvard professor proved so closely related to the argument of this present study that they demand reference. For further

---

[24] Francis Collins, *The Language of God*, New York: Free Press, 2006.

elucidation of the contents of his book, see below. Here, in this Post-script, I refer particularly to his intellectual and spiritual pilgrimage, as made known in his writings.

Seemingly he had been invited to write a paper for a learned inter-national conference to be held on the quincentenary of the birth of Copernicus to take place in 1973. As I understand the story, he was in Edinburgh at the time, so went up to the University to consult Co-pernicus's own text, *Concerning the Orbits of the heavenly Spheres*. That research produced the world-shattering publication, *The Book Nobody Read*, 2004. The title arose because Copernicus's work has been so described by Arthur Koestler, but when Gingerich searched the world for the copies still in existence, he found that all the famous mathema-ticians and astronomers had not only read the text, but had marked their text, annotated it, and written supplements. Like Saul, who in seeking to find some lost asses, stumbled into a kingdom (see 1 Sam 9-10), Gingerich found the comments and notes of Tyche Brahe the Swedish astronomer, of Kepler the German who worked with Brahe, even the notes of our own Isaac Newton. But his research at Edin-burgh is of special interest to this book.

By dint of brilliant research, Gingerich discovered that the copy he had studied at Edinburgh had been the copy that Rhetoricus had used. Rhetoricus was the young professor of astronomy and mathematics of the University of Wittenberg during the life of Luther. Rhetoricus had the distinction of persuading the aging Copernicus to have his work printed, took the precious papers back with him to Nuremberg, and finally had the emotional experience of delivering the printed sheets to Copernicus on his death bed.

The fascinating account of Gingerich's labours is there for the world to read. I must leave the story at this point, except to make two com-ments. I descend from the sublime to the desk of the student.

The first is to take note of these loving labours, and second, to re-late them to our present study.

It was following his brilliant and fascinating research on Copernicus that Gingerich was invited to give the illustrious Noble Lectures at Harvard in 2005 on Science and Religion, published in the form of a book, *God's Universe*, in 2006. In this research, we find the link with the present book. Gingerich brings the immense weight of his scien-tific learning, and writes as a scientist, pure and simple. He handles creation, Intelligent Design (which he understands as purpose, intent), and many of the issues raised in this chapter.

The reason for this postscript now emerges. In a profoundly scientific study, he concedes that for a complete understanding of existence, in its totality, physics demands and requires a *meta*physics. That complete metaphysics he finds in Jesus, and in this book quotes text from the Fourth Gospel, the very texts quoted by the present author.

The present author had arrived at the same conclusion, but by a wholly different route, namely, that of the theologian, not the scientist.

In God's work in the Incarnation of Christ, he finds his ultimate and final "Theory of Everything."

Gingerich's work lends greater weight and urgency to the contents of the present study. The present author is gratified to find such support from the eminent Harvard professor of astronomy and scientific relations. I hope that that justifies the later insertion of this postscript.

10

The Incarnation and Modern Thought

In this final chapter I shall indicate through the medium of significant, creative, informed, modern thinkers, how a reasonable, modern mind may find the true, deep significance of the Incarnation, God's Idea, an idea all have at first always resisted, even the disciples. The significance is found at two levels of experience: first, at the personal level, a way of life, what Polanyi called personal knowledge, and second, as a message for the present-day world. Both levels have been argued throughout the text. Both levels were taught by Christ.

In Chapter 7, on the difficulties of understanding and explaining religious truth, we referred to Christ's use of parable in seeking to incite or provoke to faith "all those who stood outside," i.e. those who were outside the fellowship of the disciples, who were now beginning to understand Christ's teaching. Christ sought in his teaching by parables to bring his hearers to a profounder awareness of the natural world, which they already knew and had experienced, to a spiritual understanding of their knowledge and experience, which they did not yet have. The crowds saw all these things, but did not perceive, heard all these things, but did not understand (Mk 4.11-13). The parabolic method of Jesus' teaching to the masses is a perfect expression of the integrative approach, the unitary mind, which the aesthetes, scientists and thinkers of today all pursue.

But to make a small digression (important for our argument), it furnishes a perfect example of the pastoral mind, the divine mind. Such a mind does not invade or bombard the seeking and learning mind with alien ideas or words beyond their understanding or competence, but leads them from exactly where they now are to a deeper understanding of their knowledge, from the known to the unknown.

In the mind's eye one can see Jesus teaching those crowds in Galilee with a wild anemone in his hand, a flower they had all known since childhood, picked and taken home to mother. He points out the sheer beauty of that wild flower, lovelier than any they could create or conceive, lovelier than even Solomon at his most magnificent. He was leading his listeners from their awareness of this beautiful flower to an awareness of him who had created it, a new level of thought, of him who had created them. The flower would perish tomorrow, but God had a deeper concern for them – by the very presence of Jesus.

That is one way of viewing Creation, at a religious level, as the Big Bang is another, at a scientific level. The two ways are in no way in conflict; they are simply parallel. As Gödel reminds us, nothing is fully explained at one single level of thought. The full truth needs at least two levels. The decisive thing is to apprehend and comprehend all the levels given us, not least, the ultimate one which the Incarnation proffers.

It is true to say that the "natural human"[1] who lives a normal, natural, reasonable, intelligent life may find such thinking difficult to accept. The attempt to interpret one's life by introducing a new factor, such as God or the Incarnation, or even ideas such as time and eternity, sin and salvation and the like, meets at once a natural, reasonable resistance. Even the disciples found it hard to believe Christ. One has to overcome that natural resistance by convincing oneself by reason, that reason is inadequate to explain one's normal, natural experience. For instance, in order to answer the questions one may normally or occasionally put to oneself: Why am I here? What am I? The purpose? The End? Just nothing? No! The natural human person at heart seeks and needs some rational explanation of his/her being and existence. Only religion, only the Incarnation, in whom reason (Logos) became human, and dwelt among us, taught us, redeemed us from our ignorance and sin, and left the divine dimension of the Holy Spirit to dwell with us and to lead us to the whole truth, meets our own natural problems. Our contemporaries have a harder struggle against unbelief than even the contemporaries of Jesus, for they had not suffered the secularizing influence of modern liberal education as we have.

Just as scientific knowledge is true, valid and verifiable the world over (which means that physics, chemistry and mathematics are universally true in the world we live in, perhaps even for the universe), so also is theological truth, so is Christ universally true for, and verifiable by all men, all women, all young people, all the little children. And, just as each discipline has its own canons of judgment that cannot be applied to another, and sometimes its own logic, so also theological

---

[1] By this term we mean the normal human being we meet every day, apart from any religious context or connotation. It comes from Luther's theology, *der natürliche Mensch*.

science has its own canons of judgment, even its own logic. *Mutatis mutandis*, the same may be said of music and of art, as well as poetry and literature.

Fritjov Kaptra, the world-renowned theoretical light-energy physicist, has written extensively on the philosophical implications of modern science.[2] he turns away from the mechanistic worldview of Newton and Descartes, to a view consistent with New Physics[3] to the vision of a holistic, systems-based approach in which he includes the whole living experience of modern humanity - medicine, psychology, economics, political science and ecology generated by the New Physics. He sees this unitary new creative thinking as the turning point of modern culture.

Further light on finding the meaning of things, the meaning of our life, the meaning of events in our life, the meaning of the arts and sciences, of evil and of good, of sickness and death, in short "a theory of everything," or in the words of 2 Esdras, that "candle of understanding" burning in the heart, is shed by the writings of Michael Polanyi (1891-1976) scientist, philosopher, thinker.[4]

It would be neither possible nor profitable to the reader to sum up Polyani's massive and profound work on meaning, which he entitled *Personal Knowledge*, for almost every idea he expresses, even his choice of words, creates in the reader fresh thoughts and ideas; nevertheless, it is apposite in this context of our enquiry, to indicate the major lines of his thinking.

The work in question is primarily an enquiry into the nature and justification of scientific knowledge. But, and this is important to say, any reconsideration of scientific knowledge leads on to a vast range of questions outside science.

He begins by rejecting the idea of scientific detachment outright. In the exact sciences, this false ideal is perhaps harmless enough, for it is in fact disregarded there by scientists. But he argues that it exercises a destructive influence in biology, psychology and sociology, sciences that are concerned primarily with human beings rather than with matter. It further falsified our whole outlook far beyond the domain of modern science. (It is a scientist saying these things about science, not an ignorant arts man.) he affirms that he is seeking to establish an alter-

---

[2] Fritjov Kaptra, *The Turning Point*, 1983; *The Tao of Physics*, 1976.

[3] See Chapter 9.

[4] Michael Polanyi, *Personal Knowledge*, 1958 (a heavy book, but profound and illuminating); Michael Polanyi and Harry Posch, *Meaning*, 1975 (a shorter work which sums up Polyani's life's work).

native idea of knowledge. The negative results of science and philosophy, as seen for instance in Galileo, Gassendi, John Locke and David Hume, have served to deprive us of meaning, and have resulted in agnosticism, skepticism and secularism.

He uses the findings of Gestalt psychology (a way of understanding by perceiving patterns or relationships between different ideas or objects) as his first clue to conceptual reform. He argues that scientists have run away from the philosophical implications of Gestalt. He wants to face up to them uncompromisingly. He regards knowing as an *active* comprehension of the things known, an action that requires skill. Skilful knowing and doing is performed by subordinating a set of particulars as clues or tools, to the shaping of a skilful achievement, whether practical or theoretical. We may then be said to become "subsidiarily aware" of those particulars within our "focal awareness" of the coherent entity that we achieve. Clues and tools are things used as such, and not observed in themselves. They are made to function as extensions of our faculties (bodily equipment) and this involves a certain change in our own being.[5] Acts of comprehension are to this extent irreversible, and also non-critical. For we cannot possess any fixed framework within which the reshaping of our hitherto fixed framework could be critically tested.

Such is the personal participation of the knower in all acts of understanding. But this does not make our acts of understanding subjective. Comprehension is neither an arbitrary act nor a passive experience but a responsible act claiming universal validity. Such knowing is indeed objective in the sense of establishing contact with a hidden reality, contact which is defined as the condition for anticipating an indeterminate range of yet unknown (and perhaps as yet inconceivable) true implications. It seems reasonable (he argues) to describe the fusion of the personal and the object as "personal knowledge."

Personal knowledge is an intellectual commitment, and as such inherently hazardous. Only affirmations that could be false can be said to convey objective knowledge of this kind. He says that all affirmations in his book are his own personal commitments. They claim this and are no more than this.

In his section on the Fiduciary Programme, he stresses the centrality of faith in the words "the fiduciary rootedness of all rationality"

---

[5] An illustration of this ontological change in our own being is the experience of religious conversion. We are a new creation. Another illustration may be instance by coming under the influence of a great teacher, even of a good friend, or simply falling in love with someone.

(p. 297), and goes on to say that "truth is something that can be thought of only by believing it" (p. 305). Earlier he says, quoting St. Augustine, *nisi credideritis non intelligitis.*[6] In another passage he writes, "In every act of knowing there enters a tacit and passionate contribution of the person knowing what is being known, and that this co-efficient is no mere imperfection, but a necessary component of all knowledge" (p. 312); and "to avoid believing you must stop thinking" (p. 314). This he describes as "the orthodoxy of commitment" (p. 379).

This, of course, is in the authentic Christian tradition maintained by the Church Fathers. For example, Clement of Alexandria[7] (155 - 220) in his attack on Gnosticism said, "Unless you believe, you will in no way understand," quoting Isa 7.9, Septuagint version.

Anselm (1033 - 1100) spoke, too, of the necessity of faith to understand:

> I do not try, Lord, to attain your lofty heights because my understanding is in no way equal to it. But I do desire to understand your truth a little, the truth that my heart believes and loves. For I do not seek to understand so that I may believe, but I believe so that I may understand. For I believe this also, that unless I believe, I shall not understand. (*Proslogion*, I.)

Throughout the book, Polyani has tried to make this situation apparent. He has shown that in every act of knowing there enters a passionate contribution of the person knowing what is being known, and that this coefficient is no mere interpretation but a vital component of his knowledge.

On this point he says,

> The religious hypothesis, if it indeed hold that the world is meaningful rather than absurd, is therefore a viable hypothesis for us. There is no scientific reason why one cannot believe it ... (p. 179). Religion produces a greater meaning in ourselves, in our lives, and in our grasp of the nature of all things (p. 160).

In conclusion, he adds:

> On our imperfect nature, and only by faith and trust in the all-encompassing grace of God, we project ourselves into the Kingdom of God to dwell in peace and hope. God said to Paul, "I will not remove your infirmity. For my strength is made perfect in weakness." (The reference is to 2 Cor 12.9-11).

---

[6] Unless you believe you cannot understand.

The foundation of meaning, Polanyi contends, rests on human creative ability. By use of the imagination, men and women synthesize the
otherwise chaotic and disparate elements of their lives, largely through
metaphysical expression in poetry, art, myth and religion. These kinds
of interpretation, as well as those of science, are therefore all meaningful creations accomplished by men and women through their own
imagination, participation in them and are all equally valid modes of
human knowledge.

It is Polyani's hope that this view of the foundation of meaning will
restore meaningfulness to the traditional human ideals that were un-
dercut by science. He also outlines the general conditions present in a
free society that permit people to pursue truth in their own situation
in these various ways, and includes an illuminating discussion on how
to restore to fully modern minds, the possibility for the acceptance of
religion. Polyani's attempt to free people from the shackles of objectivity and sceptical criticism stands as an appropriate final achievement - a
venture into the registration of meaning towards which all his earlier
efforts had pointed.

Around this central fact of meaning, he goes on to say, he has tried
to construct a system of co-relative beliefs which he sincerely holds,
and to which he sees no acceptable alternatives. But ultimately, it is his
own allegiance that upholds these convictions, and it is on such war-
rant alone that they can claim the reader's attention.

In the concluding words of his book he states:

> We may envisage then a cosmic field which called forth all these cen-
> tres [of thought and responsibilities in the visible world] by offering
> them a short-lived, limited, hazardous opportunity for making some
> progress of their own towards an unthinkable consummation.

And that is also, I believe, how a Christian is placed when worship-
ping God.

I referred above to the book, *Meaning* (see note 61). Its special value
for the present study is that Professor Posch wrote it conjointly with
Polyani himself, who nearing the end of his life, collaborated with
Posch to sum up his philosophic endeavours. The book, highly interesting and particularly valuable, details the development of Polyani's
thought beyond his critique of scientific "objectivity." Posch provides
a useful summary of Polyani's earlier works, which leads to the topics
of his most recent investigations: knowing is founded upon human
imagination and creative faculties, and on the sorts of meaning
achieved in metaphysics, poetry, art, ritual, myth and religion.

The authors begin with the problem of Nihilism,[8] the rise of which they attribute to the fact that traditional values cannot be verified scientifically. However, as Polanyi demonstrated in earlier works, science is not the standard of meaning but is itself a socially mediated and inherently normative form of knowledge. From this perspective, people give meaning to science instead of being given the "truth" by science.

Tom Torrance carries this view into the world of religion and theology, our present concern.[9] One could say that his main concern is in the field of theological method and theological meaning, and in the relationship between theology and science. He considers that much theology and biblical thinking has become trapped in analytical and dualist ways of thinking made obsolescent by advances in the New Physics. Instead of tearing apart "self and the world, subject and object, fact and meaning, reality and interpretation," modern science since James Clerk Maxwell (1831-79) and Albert Einstein (1879-1955) works with unitary, integrative, relational modes of thought. Thus true scientific objectivity lies not in detachment from reality (the object of study) but in a relationship to reality, in which our ideas are called in question and which we see more and understand more. Exactly as Christ called to those "outside" to see further, to hear more and so understand.

This means that in theology we begin, as any other scientist, with faith, which is a fully rational, cognitive, intuitive apprehension of reality. Reality in this case is the Lord God. The God who has himself in grace willed himself to be known in his articulate Word made flesh. God's self-revelation in Jesus is identical with God himself (for the Son

---

[8] Nihilism: This is rather a vague and wide term, which means literally "belief in nothing." It means the rejection of all moral and religious principles. Historically, the term originated in Russia during the nineteenth century, where in literary and revolutionary circles it was virtually indistinguishable from "anarchy." In eastern philosophy it may mean the denial that anything is real. But in modern thought in the West it tends to mean a philosophical outlook that directs our attention to affective states of the mind, such as boredom, cynicism, lack of concern, emptiness. We had a good example of this in the student unrest of the 1960s, with all the protest, marches, sit-ins, negative thinking, the "God is dead" movement and the like. All traditional values were mocked and flouted.

[9] See among others: Thomas F. Torrance, *Theology in Reconstruction*, 1965; *Christian Theology and Scientific Culture*, 1969; *Space, Time and Incarnation*, 1969; *Theological Science*, 1969; *The Ground and Grammar of Theology*, 1980. For the purpose of this study we restrict ourselves to his theological science, but are fully aware of his profound biblical knowledge, his wide Patristic knowledge, his complete command of Luther and Calvin, of modern theology and science, and biblical studies; see Chapter 9.

is consubstantial with the Father) so that we know God only as we are reconciled to him in Christ.

Like all sciences, theology is distinctive in developing its own peculiar logic and structures. The great dogmas of the Church, particularly the declaration of the Nicene Creed that the Son is consubstantial (*homoousios*) with the Father, are analogous to the great scientific constructs such as Einstein's theory of relativity. They are open-ended structures of thought giving insight into a reality that greatly and mysteriously transcends our knowing of it.

When theology is vigorously faithful to the truth of God's revelation, it will call in question our culture-bound formulations of doctrine, and is thus bound to be integrative and ecumenical. As integrative modes of thought gain ground, Torrance sees a massive new synthesis emerging in which all scientific endeavour is set in its theological context and man fulfils his God-given role as "the priest of creation," humbly articulating the mysterious intelligibility of the universe to the praise of its creator.

The heartbeat of Torrance's theology is the living Christ. This is the power behind his creative, visionary thinking, the consequences of which have yet to be harvested. It is an expression of what the Incarnation means for the present generation.

Concluding Reflections

The overriding purpose of the present study is to make clear the meaning of the Incarnation and its significance for modern thought.

To that end we have shown in Part I how the common people who first heard Jesus preaching and first felt his healing hand responded to his nature and his ministry, and how Jesus explained his ministry to them. We indicated how he gradually developed the insight of his chosen disciples to a profounder grasp of his mission and ministry, to a deeper understanding of his nature and being through a series of revelatory, supernatural experiences, alongside public preaching and private explanation to his disciples. These supernatural experiences were his public baptism by John the Baptist, when, as the evangelist expressed it, God intervened to confirm the nature of his Son Christ and that the people were to listen to Jesus. There were other revelatory incidents, such as the long testing in the wilderness we call the Temptation, when God confirmed him in the face of the intellectual and spiritual challenge of Satan tempting him to adopt a more sensible and realistic approach to his messiahship, the generally accepted view of Judaism. Then followed his preaching and teaching ministry, until he challenged his disciples at Caesarea Philippi, "And you? Who do you say I am?" questioning whether they truly and fully understood his real nature and being, and the purpose of his mission. Peter believed Jesus was the Christ, but was severely censured for thinking in the normal traditional Jewish expectation, and not in Christ's own divine terms to be fulfilled on a cross in Jerusalem, God's way. Then there followed that supernatural experience of the Transfiguration when the three inner disciples, Peter, James and John, actually heard Jesus in communication with God, Moses and Elijah; heard God confirm Jesus as his Son, his Messiah, to whom they were to listen. On the strength of this revelation, Jesus set his face toward Jerusalem, there to accomplish his divine mission. In short, how he had gradually led his disciples from their earlier view of him as the Messiah expected by the Jews, teacher, healer, leader, to God's Idea, the Christ, Immanuel, God with us, from Jesus to Christ.

Finally, in his last words, such was the Christ they were to offer to the whole world, the eternal, cosmic Christ, who would be with all such disciples till the end time, till God's purpose was fulfilled.

Then we turned our attention in Part I to the interpretation of Christ given by the three great theologians of the New Testament, the author of St. John's Gospel, St. Paul, and the author of the Epistle to the Hebrews. We noted how these interpretations were all worked out in the face of opposition: against all Gnostics; all Ebionites with their Judaic view of Christ; all schismatics and free thinkers; all who would measure Christ by their own way of thinking. The New Testament thinkers prevailed, as truth always must, and were later to be supported by a galaxy of great Church Fathers, and finally made authoritative by our creeds of Nicea (325) and the Definition of Chalcedon (451).

With this immense corpus of experience, learning and explanation expressed in the New Testament and Tradition, we may truly claim that Christianity is the heir of all past time and the interpreter of the future. Or, as St. Paul expressed it, all things are fulfilled in Christ.

In Part III we suggested lines on which such thinking would illuminate not only a present-day understanding of the meaning of Christ, why God sent us the Christ who actually did come, but also to create or discover what I have described as an "incarnational understanding." This enables us to experience the liberating enlightenment of a divine understanding of what is happening to us in the present world of today and to know the intense joy and immense energy that well up in our hearts and minds when we begin to understand "the mystery of Christ," "the divine purpose of history," and above all, who we are, what we are, and where we are going. Like John Bunyan, the tinker travelling from house to house mending kettles and pans, who would cry out to the rooks his better song of God's love and concern shown in Christ, I cry out to the moors. I whisper to the river, and to the woods, of this "mystery of his purpose."

In the pursuit of an Incarnational Understanding, in other words, how the Incarnation transforms and illuminates the understanding of ourselves and our place in the universe, I devoted a chapter to "understanding God's ways with humankind." I then turned my attention to the problem of understanding religious thought and religious experience, as distinct from scientific thought and everyday experience. I sought to explain Christ as the Eternal Present and what this meant for faith and discipleship, and the meaning of Church. I then moved into the vital, creative area in which cosmology and the New Physics are opening up a new way of understanding a holistic, integrative harmonizing of science and religion, and the key role that understanding of the eternal and universal Christ should play in this movement. Finally, I sought to show how such an understanding of Christ articulates for the modern man or woman, and creates in him or her a mysterious intelligibility of the universe and his or her place in it.

But I hasten to add at this point that such theological science in no way detracts from, or is a substitute for, the simple gospel experience of Christ as one's personal Saviour and Redeemer. On the contrary, it strengthens such faith. "For no one can lay any foundation other than the one that has been laid; that foundation is Jesus Christ" (1 Cor 3.11). Such a divine experience provides a total and final experience of the nature and destiny of human nature for the faithful disciple, and such may have no problems with Christian faith. The present study is a fulfilment of that Gospel of Christ to help the modern mind understand old truths, which, as truths, like scientific truths, cannot change. In addition, such theological science helps modern men and women to understand themselves in this modern techno-scientific world teeming with scientific complexities and difficulties all crying out for a theologico-cum-scientific explication.

What all this means is that once you grasp the meaning and significance of the Incarnation, or as I would prefer to express it, once the meaning and significance of the Incarnation grasps you, as God's Idea, your entire understanding of every experience, every thought, is transformed. As St. Paul expressed it:

> For our knowledge is imperfect
> And our prophecy is imperfect.
> But when the perfect comes,
> The imperfect will pass away.
> When I was a child, I thought like a child, I reasoned as a child.
> When I became a man, I gave up childish ways.
> For now we see through a mirror dimly,
> But then face to face.
> Now I know in part, then shall I understand fully. (1 Cor 13.9-12, KJV)

What St. Paul is saying is that to see and understand the significance and meaning of the Incarnation now in this mortal life is the beginning of all understanding, which can only be fulfilled and completed when in the end we break this mortal coil and meet face to face. We now understand partially, but at the end of our journey will understand fully.

I have spoken of what can only be our partial understanding, but that partial understanding is all we need now. We have begun to see with the mind of God, begun to understand. In the light of that partial understanding, I sought to illuminate the ways God is handling us. In the light of that partial understanding, which I have named an "incarnational understanding," I explained how to understand the meaning of religious truth and what discipleship and belief mean, together with commitment to Church.

I then sought to explain the existing developments in the New Physics and the essential contribution that belief in the Incarnation brings towards an integrative understanding of our being and existence. Related to this, I sought to explain what this "partial understanding" or "Incarnational Understanding" might contribute towards modern thinking in the way of a divine corrective. I have but sought to "open up to us the Scriptures" as Christ did (Lk 24.32), and does. No more, no less.

The closing words of St. Matthew's Gospel (taken literally at their face value in the present context), reveal the risen Jesus, no longer the Incarnate Christ, but in his original, permanent true nature and being, the Eternal Christ, addressing his eleven disciples, and saying to them, even though some of them still doubted,

> All authority in heaven and on earth has been given to me.
> Go therefore and "disciple-ize" (*matheteusate*) all nations,
> baptizing them in the name of the Father,
> and of the Son, and of the Holy Spirit,
> teaching (*didaskontes*) all I have taught you.
> And always remember that I am ever with you,
> to the end of time. (Mt 28.16ff.)[10]

Note very carefully, Christ states that he is not speaking on his own authority, a truth St. John reminds us of over and over again in his Gospel, but is speaking on the authority of God, the authority for all men and women the world over, of universal and eternal dominion. He speaks to all humanity at all times. He addresses his chosen disciples as the chosen of God, exalted above time and space, as the exalted eschatological ruler and judge of the world and its eternal guide. Dear reader, think on these statements. Do not start by asking yourself what they mean. Begin at the other end, and let them speak to you.

And that is what we are offering to the world. We are offering Christ, not Christianity.[11] Nor are we offering the Christian hierarchy.[12]

This is a staggering claim. Many will demur; many will resist vociferously, as many did when the words were first spoken. But they are

---

[10] This is my own rather literal translation, offered not as a better translation, but only to bring out the meaning of Christ's words for the present argument.

[11] Christianity is another category of thought, and is given honourable treatment throughout the text, as it rightly deserves.

[12] The Christian hierarchy, likewise, is a different category of thought, as is the Church. We must distinguish between the things that are different.

his recorded words, and all I have done is to make them clear. I merely seek to penetrate beyond the speech (the *lalia*) to their meaning (*logon*, Jn 8.43) as Christ intended.

It follows from this, and from Christ's own explanation of his nature and being, that he knew himself as God, "I and the Father are one" [one reality] (Jn 10.36); that, "anyone who has seen me has seen the Father" (Jn 14.9); that, he was from God, sent by God (Jn 20.19); that he was permanently with God, and would return to God (Jn 14.2-4); that his earthly life was the divine life lived within the cruel restraints of humanity (temptation, Gethsemane, the cross, the heartbreak at the heart of things); and that he saw himself as sent for the whole world to disclose these truths to lost mankind, and "As the Father sent me, so I send you" (Jn 20.21).

The *uni*verse is a single place, and needs a single idea to explain it. That single idea is Christ, God's idea. It is God who created the universe. He has given us Christ to explain it. And, at the present moment, the New Physicists are helping us to understand it, in a more comprehensive and integrative way. Together with the new understanding of the Incarnation I have sought to offer in this text, Christ as the universal, eternal One. The New Physicists will help us to disclose the full meaning of things, the "Theory of Everything."

The present author feels he can express these truths only in such terms as the universal Christ, the cosmic Christ, the Eternal Christ, the longed for "Theory of Everything," or quite simply, as it has always been expressed, the Incarnation.

No other person than Christ in all history has ever made such a claim; no other religion or culture has ever claimed this for its founder.

On divine authority, I say,

"Listen to him."

Index of Names

Index of Subjects

Index of Biblical References